AMÉRIÇAISIAN PSYCe

AMÉRIÇAISIAN PSYCe

Matthew Vandenberg

Published by Tablo

Table of Contents

Chapter 1

The assassination of an ambassador was not my usual department. I should have maybe been in a department in France. But I just had to be in Dubai, for the sake of gunnery: THAT department. I may as well have been a cabinet officer heading the Department of State, given the power I had. Instead, I was simply working for an Emirati police department, and diligently, just for a day. A day was all I needed to feel what it's like to shoot a man dead, in cold blood.

I suffered no consequences, unsurprisingly. I am a powerful Amériçaisian; more powerful than Matthew was.

Matthew Vandenberg, the late Australian ambassador to Amériçaisia, may just as well have been killed by a thermobaric weapon; a vacuum bomb, such was the lack of evidence tying me to the murder; the figurative vacuum of space suggesting the silence of someone pleading the Fifth forever. I was so perpetually high that I was like an astronaut, when staring intently at the still body of the ambassador. I saw no bullet wound, again like the vacuum bomb was employed for my objective. There was nothing unusual to see on his skin, at first cursory glance (and I indeed glanced at him cursively, tilting my head to one side). I could just imagine him struggling to breathe after his air sacs were destroyed by pressure waves, but sadly they weren't, because I only merely shot him. I can now just imagine a child suffering from a pulmonary embolism. Perhaps the embolism can even be more than pulmonary. I can imagine a little girl crying out one last time before suffering a stroke or heart attack because blood in arteries has clotted too much following the propagation of pressure waves that emanated from a fireball, through her delicate body, now limp and lifeless like tissue paper that can be arranged into the shape of a mushroom: my favorite cloud nine . . . eight . . . seven . . .

Forget about traditional explosive devices, as incredible as they are. The production of only a brief pulse, isn't even good enough to shoot in Hollywood. I need something more diabolical. In fact, I want to BE a true BALL OF FIRE.

Personally, I can relax.

My name's Hill, and I'm a lobbyist for a weapons manufacturer called Waytheon. I'm untouchable. But if I WERE touchable, I would still so wish I could be that ball of fire.

Since I was a child, I have always fantasized about the rapid shrinking of the global population; fewer and fewer people inhabiting the world, until I can personally keep track of every single person on the planet. Populaces are already shrinking away completely, while I simply shrink away from shrinks. But I never shrink away from making tough executive decisions. While Matthew was the first person I personally shot, I proudly and indirectly cause the deaths of thousands of people daily, through my indirect practices.

Hedonism is the only reason for me doing what I do. I'm sure that many other individuals in my shoes may feel morally superior to common people, but I do not labor under any such illusion. I don't think that I'm making the world a better place. I don't think that I'm helping people. If I actually AM, then I would much rather not be. I don't have any sense of cognitive dissonance when I push weapons to warmongers and psychopaths. I understand completely what I'm doing, and I willfully commit my acts. The frightening thing for many people in my active footwear (shoes) would be to come to the realization that even though they may think about things differently to me, their actions are exactly same as mine. Further, the consequences that follow all such actions, are identical. But the fact that they don't realize this, is for the best.

They must never realize this. I love what I do too much, and don't want my entire occupation to be jeopardized. Donald Trump probably understands what lobbyists like me do, all too well. He's presently in possession of classified documents that surely detail associated affairs, and that bugs me no end. What's he going to do with them? They must never appear on Wikileaks, or I'm done for.

I step into Franklin Park from K Street Northwest. I love to walk through this park to mentally rehearse speeches; phrases; praise of armaments. It's my job to convince legislators here in D.C. of the brilliance of the latest technological innovations in weaponry, so that they may propose some bills to the effect that federal expenditure on such items should be increased.

I want to look into the eyes of a victim of war one day. I want to watch the pupils of people dying before MY very eyes, like I'm an optometrist checking if they can see my favorite weapons as clear as day (but there may be clouds on the horizon). I can be a professional. I love professional advancement, career advancement, and the advancement of arms manufacturers, at the expense of social advancement, and weak people truly advancing on my position. I want as many such people as possible staring back at me all at once, unable to speak because of the unbearable pain they're all experiencing. I want them to know that it's my fault that they're in pain, but only when it's too fuckin' late for them to do anything about it, and they're crouching mute, their legs gradually giving way beneath them, like age is wearying them in record time. I want an army of people with no ARMS watching me and silently begging me for mercy with only their withering bodies. Then I want to see their limp bodies lying next to hard, glistening weaponry, and contrast their dull, lifeless, stares, with the clean, smooth, shiny metal of real arms.

Sometimes I fantasize about seeing such people right here in Franklin Park. I fantasize about a human-induced apocalypse. It's just fascinating to ponder how we're already capable of bringing one about. I like to drop a bombshell whenever I give a new speech, but I fantasize about really dropping a nuclear bomb on a country of my choice. There were people who seriously longed to see the atomic bomb get dropped on Hiroshima back in the day. They didn't want Japan to surrender, at any cost. They wanted to see just what dropping such an atomic marvel onto a populated city would do. Paul Warfield Tibbets Jr. was the man lucky enough to do the honors. But he was too far from the action for my liking.

This is why I truly wish I could BE a fireball. I want to be where people are dying, but feel nothing myself. I already know that I would feel nothing in a sympathetic sense (although an apocalyptic atmosphere would indeed be sympathetic, given that it would be in striking a[c]cord with my demeanor, like I would even be shaking sexually electrical cord-like hands with myself as Mother Nature), as much as I would still be very sympathetic to the higher power that has graciously granted me the opportunity to dwell in the wicked annihilation of my fellow men, women, and kids, and sympathetic toward such an orgy of genocide, as my sympathetic nervous system flies into overdrive, as I watch only others fight to their death to every beat of my throbbing penile heart, and independently rise above the mess I've had a wise old hand in creating so diligently and effortlessly.

I bump into an elderly Japanese woman.

'I'm very sorry, ma'am,' I state.

'At least you weren't on your phone,' the woman quips.

I smile.

I can be on a lot more than a simple cell.

******

- Christina Milian - When You Look at Me (Official Music Video)
https://youtu.be/nxRIjRSzxGo

- New Scientist
What are vacuum bombs and is Russia using them in Ukraine?
https://www.newscientist.com/article/2310098-what-are-vacuum-bombs-and-is-russia-using-them-in-ukraine/
["The fireball causes an outward pressure wave which is far more dangerous than the brief pulse produced by high explosives. It causes distinct injuries, typically in the lungs, where the pressure wave can destroy delicate air sacs or cause a massive embolism, leaving victims dead with no signs of external damage."]

- Heart
Heart Attack and Stroke Symptoms
News
Pulmonary embolism is common and can be deadly, but few know the signs
https://www.heart.org/en/news/2021/11/23/pulmonary-embolism-is-common-and-can-be-deadly-but-few-know-the-signs
["Blood clots in arteries, which carry blood from the heart, can cause heart attacks and strokes."]

- The Sydney Morning Herald
World / North America / US politics
Affidavit for raid of Trump's Mar-a-Lago property reveals concern for 'top secret' documents

https://www.smh.com.au/world/north-america/affidavit-for-raid-
of-trump-s-mar-a-lago-property-reveals-concern-for-top-secret-
documents-20220827-p5bd6n.html

- WAtoday
World
FBI says Trump mixed top secret docs with magazines and other
items
https://www.watoday.com.au/world/fbi-says-trump-mixed-top-
secret-docs-with-magazines-and-other-
items-20220827-p5bd92.html?ref=rss&utm_medium=rss&utm_source
=rss_feed

- WikiLeaks
Leaks
War & Military
https://wikileaks.org/+-War-Military-+.html

- John Pilger
Another Hiroshima is Coming... Unless We Stop it Now
http://johnpilger.com/articles/another-hiroshima-is-coming-
unless-we-stop-it-now
["Stimson later admitted that "no effort was made, and none was
seriously considered, to achieve surrender merely in order not to have
to use the [atomic] bomb".";

"The day after Hiroshima was obliterated, President Harry Truman
voiced his satisfaction with the "overwhelming success" of "the
experiment"."]

Chapter 2

The reason why Donald Trump must not become president again in 2024, is because Trump is more concerned about what's going on in Amériçaisia than what's happening in the world at large. Trump gave the orders for armed forces to leave countries. But the well-established order must not change (loose change is insignificant, unorganized, and inexact). Upper social orders must keep doing what they do best. The conduct of presidents that fall in line is of the highest order. The militarism of Amériçaisian foreign policy has far reaching consequences for people in many countries, including Russia. Amériçaisian manufacturers need to keep making weaponry for people stationed in as many areas as possible. By not allowing Amériçaisian troops to take part in any new conflict, Trump proved he was not the right businessperson to be Commander in Chief of the Amériçaisian Army.

Powerful and ordinary Amériçaisians are actually all capable of doing something to bring most wars to closes rather than climaxes, and the fact that most of them have not even tried to do much, is what delights me no end. Business as usual is perfect. Amériçaisians must never be forced to take a step back from issues concerning warfare, or take a step back from war zones. They must not put any thought into change. Trump does indeed threaten and bluster, but that's not doing enough to pretend to help people in the Third World; to ensure that more military bases are duly built, globally; to make sure that common, global civilians turn viciously cold fighters; to find ever more buyers for arms; and to punish countries who don't cooperate with imperial endeavors, by imposing sanctions on them, like those imposed on Serbia, Iraq, and now Russia. All these latter things have MY sanction, like the bombing of such countries, or the use of bombs in them.

That's why I oppose Donald Trump.

I take a bench in Franklin Park.

Back in the day, weaponry was transported from the then United States to then South Vietnam. The number of such goods (that's really so good) being transported from one country to the other increased over time. Then forces left the land, after citizens of the then United States voiced their opposition to the war, because it was dragging on and then-Americans were not victorious. Profits were no longer being made. There's such a limit to how much one can profit from a war, so it's critical that citizens support a war for as long as possible.

I'm not too concerned with profiting from the distribution of arms to countries. But there is surely a correlation between profits and destruction. That's why I push making a profit whenever I get a chance to. It's smart to convince people that they're naturally greedy, whether this is true or not. When I'm successfully plugging a new weapon, I'm feeling like a person pressing campaign buttons on a fruit machine until they're red enough to almost be nuclear. The more funds are transferred between places, the more weaponry fighters get their hands on; arms on arms on arms. With the touch of a button, people can become rich like arms. They can be everywhere and expensive. Lives are rich when people have no idea just how they'll be killed. I can imagine their rich blood penetrating my nostrils like figurative sharp minds being put to bad use, before associated smells permeate dark recesses in trenches. I can imagine uncompassionately truly taking victims in. How sharp can goods be? Eyesight be damned. I push Waytheon's penetration into new national markets, as an astute lobbyist of rare penetration. I love when defensive positions are broken through, resulting in wanton death and destruction manufacturers of WMDs dearly want; destruction that I wish my eyes could penetrate enough fog and space to see clearly, or when skeptical legislators let down their guard. I barely lift a finger, yet thanks to people of gravity, gravitation, the gravity of situations, and how serious this all is, bombs fall on people, like they're entire celestial bodies. The system that I never would dream of bucking, is almost solar, given its universality.

I remove a sheet from my pocket. I have something to say to someone. But my thoughts are all over the place like bodies surely are, somewhere far from here.

I figure that everyone, bar me, should think only about figures. They can think about women's bodies, paintings, large sums of cash, and fear dark figures who can easily be painted as combative and enemies. Figures of speech can be used to paint such bleak pictures, before weapons can be put on display before them, like rays of sunshine, and shown rising from the ashes of enemies, like cyborgs. Fighters can perfectly cut a figure. It figures that the greatest figures of history are fighters.

The expenditure of money from the Amériçaisian populace almost translates directly into the expenditure of energy on battlefields globally, until common soldiers are so aptly spent also. They get dearly cut across arms before any such expenditure on them (other arms) is cut. That's how fast they die, like as fast as an electronic transfer of billions of dollars. I want to fit in by their sides like a nurse, but dig my nails into their very every wounds far more than strictly necessary. I want them to scream in agony because when they make as much noise as heavy artillery being used, it will do them a fat lot of good, but I'll feel the opposite of what they do with their high-functioning pain receptors like such soldiers themselves. The Amériçaisian dollar is a damn strong currency. With billions of them going toward the continuance of warfare, it's no wonder people get perpetually CRUSHED; defeated; sorely disappointed; in warfare, as soldiers crush toward enemies. Waytheon truly crushes warfare. At the moment, I am only on the sidelines, like I have a sideline career. How do I get to a front line, like I'm a real frontline lobbyist, without being shot myself? I want to push goods into people; to cause extensive, elaborate(, / -)material damage to their internal organs. That will give me material to work with mentally. I want to see so many soft targets squirming on the ground as they figuratively melt away beneath a Middle Eastern sun. They might be so pathetically soft. But prices should remain as hard as fuck; the best ARMOR imaginable; of prosperity, but not for the common people. Evidence of the wrongdoing of warmongers should always remain as soft as such victims. Warmongers must all work in harness, as skills and hard technology are harnessed obsessively, to assertively, actively, and fiercely pound defenseless people, like hearts pound; like any pound's some even stronger currency. Others must have words in defense of defense(s) pounded into them, and/or peace activists should be pounded in the press so well, like getting pressed into ashes.

Now, what have I got to say for myself?

******

- Consortium News
US Militarism in Russia & Around the World
https://consortiumnews.com/2022/03/18/us-militarism-in-russia-around-the-world/
["...the United States is not solely to blame for every war, but it bears some responsibility for most of them and its people may be in a unique position to end them.";
"What the United States can do for peace is not to impose sanctions, sell weapons, train insurgents, build military bases around the world, "help" its friends, issue bluster and threats. It can only help by getting out of the way."]

- The Sydney Morning Herald
Trump lets his isolationist instincts run free with troop withdrawals

https://www.smh.com.au/world/north-america/trump-lets-his-isolationist-instincts-run-free-with-troop-withdrawals-20201118-p56fn3.html

- Newsweek
U.S.
Donald Trump Is First President Since Jimmy Carter Not to Enter U.S. Troops Into New Conflict
https://www.newsweek.com/donald-trump-first-president-since-jimmy-carter-not-enter-us-troops-new-conflict-1549037

- CNN Politics
President Trump really, really likes to make threats
https://www.cnn.com/2018/03/15/politics/trump-threats-strategy/index.html

- World Socialist Web Site
TV documentary exposes devastating toll of sanctions against Iraq
https://www.wsws.org/en/articles/2000/03/iraq-m11.html
["An adviser to Bush was quoted, explaining that the "US could not allow the overthrow of Saddam Hussein without knowing that his replacement would support American policy".";
""...Iraq may well be the blueprint for policing this new order with the weapons of sanctions and bombing." A germane point, especially given the US-led bombardment of Serbia in March last year, and its leading role in the imposition of sanctions..."]

- Republic World
Russia tells US to 'abandon futile policy of blockade and sanctions' amid war with Ukraine
https://www.republicworld.com/world-news/russia-ukraine-crisis/russia-tells-us-to-abandon-futile-policy-of-blockade-and-sanctions-amid-war-with-ukraine-articleshow.html

- AP
AP News
Russia blames Ukraine for nationalist's car bombing death
https://apnews.com/article/russia-ukraine-estonia-bombings-government-and-politics-a627f80e7a96c3b19e40e8ee95ce55fd

- Michael West Media
War Powers: immense profits for arms dealers, incalculable losses for Australians
https://michaelwest.com.au/war-powers-immense-profits-for-arms-dealers-incalculable-losses-for-australians/

- American Foreign Relations
New American Nation / A-D
Arms Transfers and Trade - The vietnam war and the nixon doctrine
https://www.americanforeignrelations.com/A-D/Arms-Transfers-and-Trade-The-vietnam-war-and-the-nixon-doctrine.html
["...the United States sent ever-increasing quantities of military equipment to the South Vietnamese army...";
"But when U.S. intervention failed to produce a quick and decisive victory, the American public turned against the war and U.S. forces were eventually withdrawn."]

- A Bus on a Dusty Road
What U. S Companies Profited During the Vietnam War?
https://abusonadustyroad.com/us-companies-profited-during-vietnam-war/
["One of the dirty U.S. secrets of the U.S. War with Vietnam is how many companies profited from the war."]

- The Guardian
Opinion
Grotesque inequality is not a natural part of being human

https://www.theguardian.com/commentisfree/2014/nov/24/grotesque-inequality-greed-human-nature-capitalism

- Terminator 2: Judgment Day (1991)
Opening (Future War) | Terminator 2: Judgment Day [Remastered]
https://youtu.be/DHKxoARmjLU

Chapter 3

My meeting today with Alexandria Ocasio-Cortez - who's rather centered (that's like some party people don't know about) - is centered around Big Tech big enough to mold the Pentagon into a hexagonal fort for defense (re shaping policies); specifically centered around the recruitment of programmers from Silicon Valley. That figurative silicon is a brittle, hard weapon for reshaping society at large. In short, hackers are needed: both tech-savvy hackers and legislator hackers like Cortez. They must be taught to hack working for the better complex, and up to military industrialists. They need to want to do this. They're presently apprehensive about such activity. It's unfortunate that they can't directly hack people to death. Still, their skills are required to maybe help others do so.

Alexandria Ocasio-Cortez, along with Rashida Tlaib and others, recently supported the allocation of seven-hundred-and-thirty-eight-billion Amériçaisian dollars to the Pentagon. Trump and Cortez indeed sometimes do my idea of the right thing.

I catch sight of AOC. She takes the scenic route deeper into my low-hanging line of sight. Resolve adorns her, like paintings of historic political figures adorn walls. My ultimate goal might be to eventually convince her to fight and die for Amériçaisia, given the large amount money she's already helping funnel into the procurement of arms, like they're MOXIE and she's man enough to go to something akin to a red planet the prime color of blood.

At present, I'm much like a casual observer. I am by no means a famous lobbyist. Such a person digs their own grave. I must low-key welcome people into my midst, like low-keying the manufacturing of arms, like keying coordinates of victims, and low-key like associated affairs so need be. AOC wouldn't be gracing me with her presence if I were as well-known as her. She wouldn't be seen dead with me if I were famous, and that's somewhat unfortunate. I want to take her ethnic hand and lead her into the arms of such dealers like the hands of an enemy on all hands, but for her to be sure that her fate is in HER hands, like she has a great hand, perhaps by chance. There's no such thing as free will, but she doesn't need to know this. She'll be crushed.

One promise of the technological age is the ever greater automation of things like bloodshed, until individuals feel as though they're living on Mars without MOXIE they'll surely soon no longer be full of when finally deflated like red balloons. See the color of Mars underfoot. Arms are, of course, a far cry from MOXIE. Their presence is almost akin to the extraction of oxygen from fighters, yet the arms are dressed up as MOXIE, like essential for survival. People accordingly yearn for such arms, like these objects for simple instrument-puppets are mothers, BEFORE the signing of instruments and prime instruments of warfare. Such mothers may wear sheep's clothing, like the ones Harlow's infant monkeys hugged, but are more like the steel-like arms they only approached for food. Little infants don't expect to be killed by Mother Warfare, until they are struggling to take any more breaths.

AOC nears me gingerly but promptly. If cameras were on drones, we could indeed be caught like bees[,] ON them. Lazy videographers - drones - may be spying on us, but how can they instead spy on civilians before taking them out? I wonder, wickedly, how they can CONTROL such DRONES from afar, and how I could maybe one day be using the controls with their blessing. The most tech-savvy creators of new infotech can one day make it possible for lobbyists like me to truly directly engage in warfare, and the thought of this sends shivers down my spine, like code that's written but immoral so much at its heart that it could be deemed genetic; like I can feel genes coding for proteins necessary for viciousness. Simple apathy breeds such incredible destruction; such holy war; such unimaginable pain and suffering, like how matter is formed from energy alone. In like fashion, my words alone can become weapons that are used to arm villains and victims alike.

AOC looks at me solemnly, like she's taking her every action seriously. This is what I'd hoped for: resolute drive. She brings so much to my table that I might lose count of prospective victims. She has the approval of radical leftists; people who may not yet die for their place of birth; people whose spirits are too free. To capture such spirits in receptacles, and consume them until drunk enough to arbitrarily wage wars, is a fantastical achievement I prize. Consensus spells the assurance of doom. I see supporters of the dealership of arms as the mirror image of victims strewn across floors on floors; civilians on pavements; civilians on civilians. Programmers are just that much better at designing a figurative mirror good enough to be used in a telescope that itself can be used to see the greatest number of hapless humans possible. Top-flight programmers can make out so many victims, like they have a birds-eye view of bloodshed until their eyes become bloodshot. I want people to celebrate alongside myself, and for as similar a reason to mine as possible. They can feel the malice toward humanity like I do, but just call it by another noun. They can all be gathered somewhere someday to celebrate deaths when supposedly celebrating lives. They can imply that shocking warfare is shorthand for freedom. I yearn for their approval, and I steadfastly refuse to change.

'Hello Hill,' AOC says.

I nod.

'Hi Alex,' I reply, so that she can feel like a man.

******

- The Economist
Business | Defence is the best offence
Can tech reshape the Pentagon?
https://www.economist.com/business/2022/08/08/can-tech-reshape-the-pentagon
["America's largest weapons manufacturers lack top-flight programmers. Silicon Valley has them in spades—but has also long displayed an aversion to battlefield technology."]

- World Socialist Web Site
Alexandria Ocasio-Cortez joins House Democrats in vote for Trump war budget
https://www.wsws.org/en/articles/2019/07/27/budg-j27.html
["The most politically significant backing for the budget—and its record $738 billion for the Pentagon—came from Alexandria Ocasio-Cortez and Rashida Tlaib..."]

- ABC News
NASA's lunch box-sized instrument MOXIE successfully makes oxygen on Mars using the Red Planet's resources
https://www.abc.net.au/news/2022-09-01/nasa-moxie-instrument-makes-oxygen-on-mars/101394288

- Sam Harris - Free Will
https://youtu.be/iA6Qc8h8ulQ
[The quote is from Free Will (2012).]

- Verywell Mind
History and Biographies
Harry Harlow and the Nature of Affection
The Wire Mother Experiment
https://www.verywellmind.com/harry-harlow-and-the-nature-of-love-2795255#

["...the infant monkeys went to the wire mother only for food but preferred to spend their time with the soft, comforting cloth mother when they were not eating. [3: a reference referred to in THIS source]"]

- Los Angeles Times
Bush Says War on Terror Led to Women's Freedom
https://www.latimes.com/archives/la-xpm-2004-mar-13-na-bush13-story.html

Chapter 4

The significance of paying people visits can't be overstated. A president can visit the United Arab Emirates and Saudi Arabia, then help push through the purchase of five-billion dollars' worth of Amériçaisian missiles by Saudi Arabia in a matter of weeks, including three-point-oh-five-billion dollars' worth of Patriot MIM-one-oh-four-E ones. Further, the UAE can get its hands on two-point-two-five-billion dollars' worth of antiballistic missiles for destroying missiles when they're close to their target. I would personally prefer that all missiles hit their targets, but luckily mistakes are made, and furthermore, over three-hundred-thousand people have indeed been killed so far in less than a decade of associated warfare. It's rather clear that certain Saudis financially aided terrorists responsible for the attack on the World Trade Center, Pentagon, and the hijacking of planes, in places far from Yemen, like over a certain east coast. Controls could not have been taken by them without financial assistance from Saudis. George W. Bush knew that people didn't need to know this, as such a revelation would have placed a cozy relationship in jeopardy. Any information that could have suggested powerful Saudis helped terrorists or extremists by giving them money, just had to be shrugged off. This is a popular dance move those in the know have had to learn, and it serves us so well. Such information must not be disseminated, like it's drugs that powerful figures have declared war on. People still don't know exactly what certain Saudis may have done. They must not get their hands on any significant associated masters. They must only get master's' in FIELDS in clouds far from where warfare is being engaged in; be content with being mere masters. Certain Saudis are profoundly influential in shaping particular policies of our Amériçaisian government, and oil from their country is forever sorely needed.

AOC is no Saudi, but I may be one for all she knows. Still, her drive and ambition shine brighter than her soul. She feels she simply must talk to me, because that's what people in her pole position do, until we hardly represent opposite poles of political ideology anymore, at least just between us. We can dance gracefully around the same pole. This political slut is putty in my hands. She'll want to be surrounded by my ARMS just to feel strong.

'I hear that a lot of people are talking to you,' AOC states, greedily taking a spot by my side.

'I'm a good listener,' I reply. 'I've got a master's in psychology. Not that that means much, really.'

'You sound like a compassionate person,' AOC says.

Being a good listener means that I don't actually speak enough for anyone to know what I sound like that well. My voice and advice are no more sound than we're presently in a sound studio and safe and sound. Still, a sound economy and sound investments will surely sound even more sound to her, given she's of sound mind and sound, given her sound political title. So, I look forward to sound devastation. I don't make a noise, though. ARMS make a noise. ("Guns don't kill people" et cetera.) Ideally, no one should make noise about not making them anymore by law. And people should forget about the noise that is data on the pitfalls of capitalism. Maybe AOC does have a little free will, but she can never express her express purpose of bringing peace to people over the impressive figurative buzz of warfare that gnaws at her indefinitely.

'I am,' I state assertively. 'I'm a voice of compassionate reason in these dark times. My ultimate goal is the destruction of global arms. Now, that may sound ironic, given that I'm dedicated to my role as a particular lobbyist. But I can assure you, Alex, that I don't like missiles.

I don't like arms; weaponry. I can't tell you how many people are dying right this very second because of the weaponry and methods employed by people like those who indeed employ people like us. But, Alex,' - I look deep into her eyes - 'I push ANTIballistic missiles. These are missiles that get FIRED INTO other MISSILES; that are used to DESTROY other MISSILES; to STOP these missiles from hitting their targets; to put an END to the destruction of infrastructure and deaths of countless civilians. I am on YOUR side, Alex.'

Just seeing her face light up when these words are uttered makes me wonder if I am in fact a high-functioning psychopath. Any associated functioning is far from low, right now. My charm is an essential aspect of the visit now being paid to me, like how the violence, suffering, and death regularly being visited upon others is an essential aspect of warfare, as AOC and I simply visit with one another.

I just nailed my short speech rather than any killers; better than any other killers ever could. Genocide is a walk in the park. Speeches needn't be long. Handshakes needn't even be firm. All that matters is making a point as good as the end of a bayonet, and then LEAVING SOMEONE'S SIDE as quickly as possible, whether in an ideal or unideal manner. This is certainly preparation for homicide; genocide; the guidance of drones into civilians. SOME CHARM is SHARP. That's hurtful eventually; witty; unethical; but easy to understand at close face value. And such an object (charm) can be used to slash skin. Associated pain is indeed sharp. Now, I must leave this area at the present time sharp.

I reach into my pocket and pull out a card I then hand to AOC. She accepts it, like it's the things she just can't change.

'Just remember me,' I state.

I stand.

'That's all you wanted to tell me?' AOC asks.

'Absolutely,' I say. 'There are many more people I need to chat to. I wish you all the best, Alex.'

I nod bye, then turn and walk away.

I head deeper into Franklin Park.

Pretending to be formally giving people a hand is the oldest trick in the book. Pretending that hands hardly get strewn across grounds anywhere because of the use of ANY missiles, is an art in itself, like finger-pointing; pointing the finger at as many OTHERS as possible. I can imagine those fingers strewn across lands of free people; fingers that have truly been freed; that are not being used for good; anymore.

Money is the root of all secrecy. Were it not for money everything would be out in the open, from bloodshed to statistics. That would be a worry, since common folk aren't like me. They would wonder why the limbs of humans have to be blown off before the ownership of cities can change hands, and why hands must seemingly be EXchanged for others as wrists are severed from forearms when bombs and landmines go off as often as fruit, vegetables and meat like human flesh. It's fine for me to see someone spill their BEANS like oil, like exhuming bodies or evidence, or people exuding blood or fear, but others may not take so kindly to this.

Defensiveness is anxiousness as much as actions taken to ensure survival. But the more sides weaponry ends up in the hands of, the less certain certain people may be that such survival is possible. I can fully picture pathetic populaces growing more and more anxious, confused, and indecisive, while inanimate arms grow out of talk of pride, like businesses, turnover, and cities growing ever larger. Heads grow ever bigger, along with necks that victims and dealers alike stick out. A chopping block is the choppy seas of terrestrial warfare; a chopping block party; orgy. Everyone on some BLOCK is ready for some action. Terror inevitably rains down on them as sure as day turns into night. They suffocate under the blanket conventional wisdom of warfare. Powerful people have money to burn like victims. Weaponry provisions trump food, without prosecutions under the provision of an act banning warfare. The calm demeanor of those responsible for the smart provision of services, that belies death, completely belies criticism.

I stroll on with my head held high.

******

- The Killers - Land of the Free
https://youtu.be/OIT0ucf_gys

- This Is F*cking Crazy
https://youtu.be/obpqJ3hleAA

- Common Dreams
Weeks After Biden Fist-Bumps Saudi Prince, US OKs $5 Billion in Gulf Arms Deals
https://www.commondreams.org/news/2022/08/02/weeks-after-biden-fist-bumps-saudi-prince-us-oks-5-billion-gulf-arms-deals
["...the Biden administration's approval of more than $5 billion in missile sales to Saudi Arabia and the United Arab Emirates, a move that came weeks after U.S. President Joe Biden visited the leaders of both countries...";
"...the U.S. State Department approved the $3.05 billion sale of 300 Raytheon Patriot MIM-104E missiles to Saudi Arabia, as well as 96 Lockheed Martin Terminal High Altitude Area Defense (THAAD) missiles worth $2.25 billion for the UAE.";
"...anti-war voices argued that such sales will only prolong a seven-year war in which more than 300,000 people have been killed..."]

- The Intercept_

9/11 and the Saudi Connection

https://theintercept.com/2021/09/11/september-11-saudi-arabia/

["Mounting evidence supports allegations that Saudi Arabia helped fund the 9/11 attacks."]

["Immediately after the attacks, the Bush administration downplayed the Saudi connection and suppressed evidence that might link powerful Saudis to the funding of Islamic extremism and terrorism. The Bush White House didn't want to upset its relationship with one of the world's largest oil-producing nations, which was also an American ally with enormous political influence in Washington, and much of what the FBI discovered about possible Saudi links to the attacks remains secret even today."]

- History

September 11 Attacks

2. Osama bin Laden

https://www.history.com/topics/21st-century/9-11-attacks

["The 19 terrorists easily smuggled box-cutters and knives through security at three East Coast airports..."];

"Soon after takeoff, the terrorists commandeered the four planes and took the controls..."]

- Vice

The War on Drugs Show

https://www.vice.com/en/topic/the-war-on-drugs-show

- "Guns Don't Kill People, People Kill People": And Other Myths About Guns and Gun Control (2016)

- Psychology Today

This Charming Psychopath

https://www.psychologytoday.com/au/articles/199401/charming-psychopath

- Forbes

Healthcare

How To Accept the Things You Cannot Change, Like the Pandemic

https://www.forbes.com/sites/jessicagold/2020/07/20/how-to-accept-the-things-you-cannot-change-like-the-pandemic/?sh=8a61edb4ac76

Chapter 5

I could have arranged a meeting with Marjorie Taylor Greene, but I feel like I won't get anywhere with her. She isn't fond of the reputable people who work for the prestigious FBI. Nor does she want Ukraine to be given forty-billion Amériçaisian dollars. This republican's a peacenik activist stuck in her deviant ways. Rather, I believe that the weak, malleable, pop, socialist Squad, to which AOC belongs, are more likely to approve laws in favor of funding warfare and the Department of Homeland Security. AOC is happy for that cool forty billion bucks to reach Ukraine's bloodstained hands. Now, right-wingers absurdly oppose proxy warfare, in Congress. They don't want people to be given bucks and arms, but I truly do. See, I want them ALL to die.

Legislators must have PROGRESSIVELY LOUD VOICES to get people's attention. Opinions should be strongly HELD, like arms in arms, as people progress dangerously and perilously toward a front line, like peace is only ever possibly achieved through staunch warmongering. Associated sounds must become ever more deafening. Any party advocating this, however unknowingly, may enjoy my support, especially if rather progressive in the minds of supporters, like I enjoy career, social, and physical advancement insofar as this spells carnage. Bursts can precede bursts of activity; from citizens; of eardrum after eardrum, like ears are burning after being stabbed, and all because powerful people love hearing their names yelled out.

I peer around at the life that surrounds me, and can only fantasize about it being razed to the ground. Much to my contentment, warfare is fashionable when masquerading as security. Security seems sensible, even when tight like chests after the inhalation of smoke from a warzone. The constriction of ARMS truly all around citizens, in chests and stomachs, mirrors that of those pushed by the likes of people like me. Cold robotic steel snakes can be like a cold snake like me. Somehow, constrictions are welcome. Citizens freely fight to their death; for their imaginary country. There should be no space between people and blunt weaponry; no life about. There is a need for only instruments, automation, and CLEAR, STARK CARNAGE. The ashes of this must be FINE enough to fill the air that's somewhat ironically-freely still breathed. Such carnage can be obvious, unpleasant, absolute, severe, and simple, and citizens stark dead. These must be stark facts, and landscapes as stark as fields of dry, smoldering ruins as striking as smoldering malice.

A man several meters ahead of me is using a cane. He could be doing so for any number of reasons related to warfare. He could be ill, blind, or simply old. I imagine his gorge rising like his cane or food from below that he may reluctantly gorge on, when falling to the ground he can't possibly see, like into arms at a landfill.

I need to make my way over the figurative dead of old citizens. Citizens can be dead like areas can be; like nerves; voices; talk about limiting warfare; silence! I can walk all over people, and must. I can maliciously find my way into every bleeding heart, with the blunt heels of my feet. Will people feel THUMPS? I can PUT MY FOOT DOWN without even arousing suspicion, and push arms deep into hearts and minds, like every fuckin' thing is radical solid material. That's cool. Radical steps and parties can seem progressive so that support is expertly garnered, until bodies are being repeatedly pushed against radical tubers six feet below the ground. Change must be this radical; this forceful; this pressing, if it's to be for the ultimate worse; the greater bad. I want to feel guts beneath my soles; to sink into bodies like citizens of countries sink into comas, or dreadful carnage sinks into their minds, crippling them blind; spelling suffering from PTSD. That's disturbingly crippling. Seeing carnage is SO horrifying. It truly is. And even when blind, experiences alone can leave such citizens extensively traumatized.

Citizens can fight by using weaponry like canes, and be blindly fighting until death do they merely figuratively and spiritually TURN AROUND and walk away.

I like when people gasp for air like they gasp for soft drinks; when a price has ostensibly been put on oxygen, and it's unaffordable for the masses.

Whom can I talk to next about no such thing?

******

- This is Shameful

https://youtu.be/9YmrVAIZsDE

["...this representative Marjorie Taylor Greene denounce the FBI or denounce sending $40 billion to Ukraine. And then you see self-identified socialist lawmakers like Alexandria Ocasio-Cortez and the members of this, like, de facto progressive boy band known as The Squad, when they are voting for the 40 billion to Ukraine . . . voting for the department to fund the Department of Homeland Security . . ." - Max Blumenthal / Journalist, Author, and Blogger;

". . . like anti-war, like, you have right-wingers: the only people in Congress who are voting against funding this insane proxy war in Ukraine . . ." - Max Blumenthal / Journalist, Author, and Blogger]

- American Psychiatric Association

What is Posttraumatic Stress Disorder (PTSD)?

https://psychiatry.org/patients-families/ptsd/what-is-ptsd

["Posttraumatic stress disorder (PTSD) is a psychiatric disorder that may occur in people who have experienced or witnessed a traumatic event..."]

Chapter 6

The deeper into Franklin Park I venture, the more I imagine being underwater; submarining; submarining under submarines; or controlling such a vessel underwater. Four-thousand-six-hundred vessels were sunk using subs during World War Two. However, simple mines are often fatally OVERLOOKED, whether seen or not. Two-thousand-one-hundred vessels were sunk after mines blew up during this period. I want mines to be wholly mine. Mines were the destruction of more vessels than weaponry on ships or aircraft. People forget about how great they are for cruel crews and killers at sea. The cost of safely destroying such mines is astronomical, while the cost of deploying them is pleasingly minimal. They're so beautiful and smooth, like deaths, my manners, and like I personally am, when meshing with legislators. Pushing mines shouldn't be too hard, just like pushing further into Franklin Park; a stroll in the park.

My next endeavor will be the PLUGGING of mines. That almost sounds like a peaceful practice. Here in Washington, D.C., it is a rather local one. Benches here are quite like market stalls: it's not hard to believe that people figuratively run them. Mine will be no exception. When such people take a seat, it seems to actually be theirs for a while. The mines that I'm ultimately trying to sell to people all around the world are not on me, obviously, or I'd be DEAD MEAT, but I am capable of so expertly alluding to them that they can fill or fire the imagination of anyone I encounter. It is, however, probably easier to imagine mutilation and deaths as a result of the use of LANDmines. I do.

I take a seat before the next Amériçaisian representative to approach me. I look about and spot him. He's not quite before me yet. I was expecting to meet with Mark Meadows, but Dwight Evans is walking toward me. That's fine. Both of them, and/or their spouses, can surely afford to invest more than a paltry fifty-thousand Amériçaisian dollars in defense stocks, as they already have. Evans is invested with the great power to help make laws. That's more significant than a paltry fifty grand in investments. Evans' net worth is over a million Amériçaisian dollars as of twenty-eighteen, and Meadows' worth is now probably around thirty-million Amériçaisian dollars.

Mines are cheap. They cost spare change to folk like Mark and Dwight. I can only imagine the damage they can do if they put MY mind to it. By the power vested in me, I can pronounce them "brothers in arms". Such devices, when I'm left to my own (mine), can be tossed out to sea willy-nilly. People may do so willy-nilly (whether they like it or not). This spells destruction and carnage AT THE DROP OF A metallic HAT.

I can only hope dearly for fanfare when the representatives figuratively play with fire well enough to excite constituents. People can play with mines for the sea, like kids play in fields after perhaps peacefully moving cows about and before unexploded ordnance or landmines go off. They're more active than cows, but no less like meat when dead. ARMS can be all over the place, including at sea. The beauty is that even kids can ostensibly afford to play with such devices.

I can imagine watching ships blowing up. Blood is thicker than water, so to be on a waterfront watching a family get blown up would really be like being in the thick of it. If only properties on Stayz could afford me such wicked indulgence. The greatest BONDS can be destroyed so efficiently. Agreements also hardly matter. Mines will get deployed at sea regardless of what I may agree to. My kind promises will always be solemnly broken. I crave the craven commitment to my cause. I love cravenness like my own.

Dwight takes the space next to me. We exchange glances.

'I hear that you like bringing wars to a close,' Dwight says.

'Absolutely,' I lie. 'People do not realize how effective letting mines get buffeted by waves is as a means to this end. Mining is crucial. Think about ultimately calm seas. There can be so many waves that people won't even know what hits them.'

I give the impression that wheels are already in motion; that talk on mines are waves already well OVER PEOPLE'S HEADS; that nothing can be done to stop any associated carnage. I don't mention that mines are static, because then my friend here may get the idea of just sitting on his cash and doing nothing substantial. Seas are naturally rough, so perhaps deploying mines on them precedes the CREATION of nothing but natural WAVES. I can imagine dotting seas with figurative metal pebbles to be figuratively kicked by boats, like they're soccer balls used to unite the world. Countries can FIGHT OVER THEM, fearful of both man and what's man-made, before water ultimately overwhelms vessels, like an army otherwise might. That's CAPITAL capitalist competition I surreptitiously push. It's serious and fatal. It's professionally using the entire horrific element of water as a force for bad. Citizens might see it coming up, and know that they have nowhere to go. Then so many FEET can GET IN DOORS, but likely in different ways. I'm impatient beyond belief. Deploying mines at sea is a way for FEET to GET IN DOORS sooner, before two ships even approach each other. I deliver a crash course in mining, sure, but vessels needn't even be on a collision course with others. Time is precious. If they could all rise up AT ONCE, then this would be magical, but I'll settle for individual vessels blowing up one by one by mine by mine, rather than at the same time; now. What's mine is mines. I'm certainly selfish.

This could all sound like a revolution, but it's business as usual. People may put up their hands, but are completely powerless to change their fate; going well under like ships. There's nothing much to see at sea. Mining is standard practice. I pray that people don't watch out for mines. I would watch out for them differently if I were near such mines, like watching whales, and watching out for no whole figure. Maybe it's great to see jumpy people watch out for mines. I could one day be so excited that I jump higher than said jumpy people, just to see them off to their deaths, as citizens see off foreign citizens, and vice versa, just as easily.

'I see,' Dwight says. 'And there is growing interest in such practices?'

'There's growing interest in finally bringing wars to their necessary closes ASAP,' I state. 'The urgency of this cannot be overstated.'

I am hoping that this does not bring to Dwight's mind the nuclear bomb, but that's certainly what I think about: enough mines FANTASTICALLY and figuratively splitting the atoms of the very water that covers the majority of our planet's surface. That would be perfect, strange, beyond imagination, out of this world, and BLOODY water would be HARD TO FATHOM. I would personally rather just see blood and BLOODY people; murderous citizens; nationalists of any country; bloody mines and body parts. I would love a bird's eye view of such wonders of warfare. If enough mines are deployed at sea, then maybe the seas can become extensions of land. That's more land to fight over; to bombard; more BLOODY maniacs to watch. After bodies of bodies die, tangles of bodies can form over water, so that new terra firma is created, after citizens have first tangled with one another.

THE BOTTOM LINE is profits from the selling of mines. It's ever unaffordable to destroy them safely, as the more that are sold and deployed, the more unaffordable this becomes.

People may not drown at sea, but fantastically choke on their own blood. I can help turn oceans into blood, like a psychopathic Jesus.

Bloody water is hard with iron, almost like land, and not easy to swallow, like a whole disaster, unless I can be there to watch on as people wave at me like I'm the new king of realms. Die, loyal SUBJECTS, die. I really want to see what harm a mine can do. I love experimentation. But I should PUSH lifeboats too, because I want people to be dying as long as possible. This avenue of deception, that's almost like a solid road over water, could be a POLITICAL lifeboat. And they can hit mines too. Maybe smaller mines can be hit by smaller boats. I could almost be describing a magnificent fractal of death now.

'I agree,' Dwight says.

I smile.

******

- Dire Straits - Brothers in Arms
https://youtu.be/jhdFe3evXpk

- The Economist
Science & technology | Naval mines
Mines are the neglected workhorses of naval strategy
https://www.economist.com/science-and-technology/2022/08/31/mines-are-the-neglected-workhorses-of-naval-strategy
["They are cheap to deploy and expensive to get rid of"]
["During the second world war, these static underwater bombs are reckoned to have sunk 2,100 vessels. Not as many as the 4,600 accounted for by submarines, but far more than attacks by aircraft or artillery bombardment by other ships."]

- Kurdpa
Kurdistan Press Agency
News / Kurdistan / Human Rights / Latest News / Hot Topics

A Kurdish Kolbar was mutilated by a landmine at the Hawraman border

https://kurdpa.net/en/news/a-kurdish-kolbar-was-mutilated-by-a-landmine-at-the-hawraman-border

- Phys.org

Other Sciences \ Other \ Political science

Deaths from landmines are on the rise, and clearing them all will take decades

https://phys.org/news/2021-11-deaths-landmines-decades.html

- The American Prospect

Money, Politics and Power

The Members of Congress Who Profit from War

Serious Conflicts of Interest

Reps Invested in Top Defense Stocks

Rep.

Max Amount of Investments

https://prospect.org/power/the-members-of-congress-who-profit-from-war/

["Stocks are owned by the representatives, their spouses, or jointly."]

["Dwight Evans";

"Mark Meadows"]

["$50,000";

"$50,000"]

- Open Secrets

Candidates & Officeholders / Personal Finances / Dwight Evans (D-Pa)

Dwight Evans

See Data About Their:

Personal Finances

Select a year:

2018

https://www.opensecrets.org/personal-finances/dwight-evans/net-worth?cid=N00038450&year=2018

["...with an estimated net worth of $1,354,524 in 2018."]

- CAKnowledge.com

Net Worth » Politics

Mark Meadows Net Worth is $30 Million (Forbes 2022) Salary Assets Wealth

https://caknowledge.com/mark-meadows-net-worth/

- Relief Web

Myanmar

An Ongoing Danger: Death and injury due to landmine and UXO explosions in Southeast Myanmar form January 2020 through January 2021

B. UXO incidents

i. First Incident

https://reliefweb.int/report/myanmar/ongoing-danger-death-and-injury-due-landmine-and-uxo-explosions-southeast-myanmar

["...a local schoolchild, joined three other children who had taken their cows out to graze and were playing in the fields."]

- France 24

The Observers

Iran's landmines: 'Kids get blown up while playing'

https://observers.france24.com/en/20140407-iran-landmine-children-injured-kurdistan

- Stayz™

https://www.stayz.com.au

Chapter 7

I remove a card from my pocket and offer it to Dwight.

He accepts it, taking it in his hand.

I have nothing more to necessarily say. He's putty. I only need to be a card in order to cut across his mental guard.

I nod and rise to leave, like I have places to be.

The Amériçaisian state-sanctioned overthrow of fifty governments may take nearly one hundred years, but I can't just forever be sitting back and doing nothing in this single significant year. Democracies, especially, must be overthrown carefully, and such aforementioned governments were mostly democratic. Powerful Amériçaisians played a significant role in pushing parties, and/or doing more, during thirty ostensibly democratic elections. People in thirty countries who were mostly vulnerable and who had little money, were bombed under the orders of powerful Amériçaisians. We're that big. Heads of state of fifty countries were almost taken out by us. We did everything we could to stop people rising up against rulers in twenty countries. But I'm so good at rising up, and no one stops ME.

'That's all?' Dwight asks.

'I've gotta run,' I say with a nod.

I turn away from Dwight and simply walk, like I even lie in my sleep-walking.

I always make out that I need to see countless people. The truth is that I don't NEED to see too many. They could be citizens of a democratic country, sure, but if it's a CORPORATE democracy then only certain people truly matter. War matters, so that such people get rich quick like an explosion. Sociopathic socialists rule over poor traditional capitalists. The greatest terror attack to ever impact Amériçaisia, was significantly financially impactful for those with military-industrial stocks. Blood money was soon everywhere, and there will always be more where that came from. "Forever wars" in Yemen, Ukraine, Iraq, Palestine, and Libya, are sources of income that are the present foundation of our great forever nation. I and others cheerfully say anything and everything to ensure there is no end to the windfalling bombs over poor people. An Amériçaisian president can freely steel billions from Afghan banks, and then blame all suffering on the Taliban. That's so blame shifting, it's like me getting up and running off so suddenly. You can hear about Afghanistan on the radio for a couple hours, but only half a minute of talk about how Afghans need food. Through NATO, powerful Amériçaisians committed themselves to a plan to make sure Europe has plenty weaponry, effectively egging China and Russia on. Some greater nuclear war than ever, against such foes, has been placed on the table powerful and relaxed Amériçaisians have their feet firmly on. The West must fear Beijing, and mainstream newscasters play their role well to this end, being practically second to none others who don't push associated Sinophobic propaganda. I hope to one day travel from Amériçaisian base close to China to Amériçaisian base close to China to visit some four hundred of them situated on land by the Pacific Ocean, where the prospect of peace is ironically laughable, and notably in Australia, Japan, Southeast Asia, and Korea. I want to see the guns directed at bustling urban China, on Jeju Island and in Okinawa. We have China circled, and I'm ready to play my part in helping lynch any race I can.

Furthermore, ordinary western citizens hear that Israelis and Palestinians all have important stories to tell about the two sides of the conflict, even though many Israelis treat Palestinians the way Nazis treated Jews, taking out their anger toward the late Hitler on innocent Palestinians. These psychopaths are truly my idols. They can treat Palestinians however they like and get away with it, doing Hitler proud. Any associated OCCUPATION is beautiful. I love all my time on Earth. Sadly, we Amériçaisians can't watch Yemenis get slaughtered national television, because the mainstream media is silent on such genocide. Actually, that's a good thing. Let Amériçaisian cluster bombs controlled by Saudis with the help of Brits, fall on as many innocent souls as imaginable, behind closed doors of geography. Let five hundred thousand Yemeni children starve to death. Just let me see their creepy and deformed faces.

I'm so excited that I'm about to sadistically come.

This is the feeling that my powerful walks and liaisons between politicians and I, have been building up to, like they're powerful sexual liaisons.

I'm shaking.

My penis is throbbing.

Suddenly I'm deaf.

I'm floating in space.

I can't breathe, but maybe I'm just autoerotically high.

THWOOOOOOOSH!

Now, the ground below my feet is shaking.

Where am I?

'Mmmmm mmm,' someone says.

I think I'm in a room.

I can hear that I'm in a room.

'Mmmm mmmm,' someone repeats.

I can hear indistinct murmurs.

Where am I?

Please stop making noise. People, please weed out noise. I only want to hear about . . . um . . . Maybe I don't want to hear anything. Be quiet. Everybody's making too much noise, and about things I can't imagine. I hate noise. I hate noise unless I'm painting pretty pictures of warfare for people. I need PEACE. No. Yes. Really? I need silence.

I feel like I'm dreaming, but I'm in intense pain. I can't open my eyes. I can see a room, but I know that it's in a dream. I'm surrounded by black flames.

I can't see the people whom I want to see dead. I can't see the civilians whom I want the bombs to globally obliterate.

Arrrrgh! I cannot move an inch of any part of my body. I'm paralyzed.

I try to mentally watch a bomb falling toward children near me, but it seems to be falling onto ME. It's hard to picture devastation without being in intense and prolonged pain; a victim myself. But I want to WITNESS true suppression of human rights and riots.

I can't speak. I've always suppressed my own psychopathic free speech and emotions. Now they truly are suppressed beyond my control.

I imagine that I'm a scared little child, watching in fearful wonder as a bomb appears to grow ever larger. It's falling closer and closer to me, as dying immature life flashes before my sharp eyes that may be inside out. I can gasp, but I think I'm more in pain than ecstasy. How is that possible? Why can't I see what I so need to see? Where can I go? I'm stuck. I need to see more people around me; a hand or many hands to fly at my face. But if I'm that scared child then I want to see myself blown to pieces right before my eyes, like I'm having an out-of-body BLAST of an experience.

Stability ultimately requires warfare. I would fall apart like Amériçaisian society might were it not for others being blown apart. Weaponry is the udders that lambs need to suck on. I only feel whole when whole arsenals of hot weaponry are on callous fighters; at the disposal of warring factions. It should be so easy for ordinary citizens globally to get their filthy hands on such powerful devices.

I can imagine people on the floor of a stock exchange, jumping for joy as a bomb goes off, moving like they're victims of warfare. Perhaps a civil war could even break out between rich socialists and poor capitalists, like skin on skin on fire. That could break out bad. The more I figuratively SEE, like carnage to experience, the more I wish that dying tools were as close as a reflection in a mirror held up to my face. I want to see as many people as possible rot to death from the effects of warfare; from the face in; from one end of what they put on (like a face, an item of clothing, or/and foundation) to the other. I don't want to see brave people, but skittish folk not knowing just which way to turn one last time. I should never have to wait forever for "forever wars", because I just must have front-row seats to the carnage that must forever be what politicians pretend not to run on, when ever after dependent tickets to foster professional relations that precede further enabling of glorious gory warfare. If tickets could speak then they could maybe be raised and ask questions. Pretending to listen to voters is vital. That's why running on weak tickets of a party promoting peace, that may get ethical people's attention, is just the ticket.

I would feel so free on paper planes made of blood money, to watch warfare from above foreign lands, if not so tortuously uncomfortable right now. Why are my physical movements so restricted? They're more than restricted. Have I been arrested; I arrested? Outer happenings cannot even arrest me, but sounds are strikingly and horrifyingly deafening and piercing.

The silencing of peaceniks would certainly fill me with a joy that would mirror that of present silence. I can imagine the taping up of open mouths; the restriction of breathing sighs of relief to speak freely about bringing warfare to an end using weak stems of flowers like simple counterarguments I don't even have to put an effort into making; like weak and boring arms; like weak smiles as people brace themselves for imminent death. Weak lights at the ends of millions of personal tunnels can get dimmer and dimmer, until the dark equivalent of floodlights figuratively darken their short times left on Earth, and intense negative emotions darken their already forlorn faces. There might be no code that they can use to call for help, if lights are so romantically dim for dates with Death. The powerful MEDIA for warfare is everywhere, like air. People could live in such a medium, like simple organisms worth nothing. The happiest mediums spell death.

I need to rise and shine, but DARKNESS is all I can possibly be truly cognizant of.

'He was rushing toward the baby to save her from feeling the full force of the blast,' someone says.

Who?

I hope they didn't make it.

******

- Metallica: One (Official Music Video)
https://youtu.be/WM8bTdBs-cw

- American Psycho [- D12]
https://youtu.be/mS5LjGCe0c8

- JohnPilger.com
Silencing the Lambs. How Propaganda Works.
http://johnpilger.com/articles/silencing-the-lambs-how-propaganda-works-
["In my lifetime, the United States has overthrown or attempted to overthrow more than 50 governments, mostly democracies. It has interfered in democratic elections in 30 countries. It has dropped bombs on the people of 30 countries, most of them poor and defenceless. It has attempted to murder the leaders of 50 countries. It has fought to suppress liberation movements in 20 countries.";

"In our systems of corporate democracy, war is an economic necessity, the perfect marriage of public subsidy and private profit: socialism for the rich, capitalism for the poor. The day after 9/11 the stock prices of the war industry soared. More bloodshed was coming, which is great for business. Today, the most profitable wars have their own brand. They are called 'forever wars': Afghanistan, Palestine, Iraq, Libya, Yemen and now Ukraine. All are based on a pack of lies.";

"Today, the news from Afghanistan is how evil the Taliban are - not that Joe Biden's theft of $7 billion of the country's bank reserves is causing widespread suffering. Recently, National Public Radio in Washington devoted two hours to Afghanistan - and 30 seconds to its starving people. At its summit in Madrid in June, Nato, which is controlled by the United States, adopted a strategy document that militarises the European continent, and escalates the prospect of war with Russia and China. It proposes 'multi domain warfighting against nuclear-armed peer-competitor. In other words, nuclear war.";

"News about China in the West is almost entirely about the threat from Beijing. Airbrushed are the 400 American military bases that surround most of China, an armed necklace that reaches from Australia to the Pacific and south east Asia, Japan and Korea. The Japanese island of Okinawa and the Korean island of Jeju are loaded guns aimed point blank at the industrial heart of China. A Pentagon official described this as a 'noose'. Palestine has been misreported for as long as I can remember. To the BBC, there is the 'conflict' of 'two narratives'. The longest, most brutal, lawless military occupation in modern times is unmentionable.";

"The stricken people of Yemen barely exist. They are media unpeople. While the Saudis rain down their American cluster bombs with British advisors working alongside the Saudi targeting officers, more than half a million children face starvation."]

- Heartbreak High (2022)
Series 1
6. Angeline
[Quinni responds interestingly to noises.]

- Northwestern
Early Intervention Research Group
For Parents
Sound Sensitivity and Autism
https://ei.northwestern.edu/sound-sensitivity-autism#:~:text=Hyperacusis%20(say%20it%20with%20me,for%20your%20child%20to%20hear.

["Hyperacusis (say it with me: HY-per-uh-CUE-sis), is an increased sensitivity to sound that is commonly found among people with autism."]

- TV Tropes
Pre-Explosion Buildup
https://tvtropes.org/pmwiki/pmwiki.php/Main/
PreExplosionBuildup
["But there's a split second of intense quiet, together with the feeling of being in a vacuum, unable to take a breath; then there's the huge sound of the explosion, momentarily deafening you, making the ground tremble beneath your feet..." - Michael Korda / Journey to a Revolution]

- Journey to a Revolution: A Personal Memoir and History of the Hungarian Revolution of 1956 (2006)
[p. 167]

- Independent
Lifestyle > Health & Families > Health News
Health: When masturbation can be fatal: The practice of auto-erotic asphyxia is often concealed by a coroner's verdict. Monique Roffey looks at a lethal taboo
https://www.independent.co.uk/life-style/health-and-families/health-news/health-when-masturbation-can-be-fatal-the-practice-of-autoerotic-asphyxia-is-often-concealed-by-a-coroner-s-verdict-monique-roffey-looks-at-a-lethal-taboo-1484619.html

- TH: Traditions Health
Blog
What Does a Coma Feel Like?
Dream-like State
Can Your Loved One Hear You?
https://www.traditionshealth.com/blog/what-does-a-coma-feel-like#:~:text=A%20coma%20is%20similar%20to,or%20communicate%20in%20any%20way.
["A coma is similar to a dream-like state because the individual is alive but not conscious."]

["However, the brain may still be able to pick up on sounds from loved ones."]

- Sleep Foundation
Sleep Disorders / Parasomnias
What You Should Know About Sleep Paralysis
https://www.sleepfoundation.org/parasomnias/sleep-paralysis

Chapter 8

I feel as though there is hardly any point to WAKE-UP CALLS. I'm still asleep. I know that I'm dreaming, but I just can't possibly wake up no matter how many people may be calling out my name or calling me. Furthermore, I can't tell if Japan's army is presently growing in strength, given the fighting going on in Ukraine that warmongers like to call a wake-up call for such peaceful Asians. Last I heard, Japanese people dearly want arms or want an army of theirs to have ever more. I'm meant to be meeting with Japanese men or women. But I can't move. I needed to talk to Mark Takano. Or was I going to chat to Mazie Hirono or Doris Matsui? I can't recall whom I was meant to see next. I wanted to talk to Mark about how an arsenal of Native veterans needed an arsenal of advice on being confident in their ability to use arsenals. They would have deserved all the weaponry that they could and should have been given when serving in the armed forces. That may sound like the pushing of weaponry though. I still need to work on my speech. The focus of Native veterans should certainly have been on killing enemies, rather than now on killing themselves and mentally suffering, because it's hard to see when they are suffering. And I WANT to see people suffer. They sure need help, but I need to keep Mark from doing anything to stop them from experiencing anguish and taking their lives, because they will only want to go on to criticize warfare. Or I could be next chatting to Mazie Hirono about her excellent use of violent rhetoric I could personally employ. The prohibition of abortions angers her so much that I could surely convince her that supporters of abortion in faraway places require weaponry to defend their human rights. I love calls to ARMS babies can be held in. I could also be chatting to Doris Matsui about the importance of reading up on the remarkable new arms being produced, for the sake of literacy. Inclusion, on top of everyone being able to benefit from equal access to associated digital learning, is crucial. Engendering a feeling of inclusion is, after all, key to recruiting people into the armed forces.

Why can't I move? I can't even move my eyelids.

'He's a hero,' someone says.

Who?

'She survived because of him,' this someone continues.

I guess that if I could speak then I would want to pretend that I care; that it's great that some baby didn't die. But I can only stay silent.

Am I in a coma?

I must love this person who's talking, or learn to.

This is insane.

Can't they shake me awake? How HARD can that be? Have they checked my vital signs? I would say that's presently vital.

'It was free-will provision of aid,' someone states.

I never believed in free will, but now it's blatantly obvious that I have NO free will whatsoever. I don't know what this person's going on about.

Japanese people need to be groomed for warfare; to fight others using magnificent arms. I can imagine grooming them for warfare now, because I imagine people are looking at me now, gazing down at me like I'm a baby in a crib, helpless like a crip or Crip in the wrong crib. I can almost imagine being these people watching over me but doing more than simply staring at someone who's helpless: instead, angering babies or toddlers; infuriating infants; raising them like rebellions; like fears that foreign people are out to hunt them down; raising them to fight until their death. That's a life like that in service to royalty. I can imagine weaponizing cutesy Akihabara; raising young Japanese girls to slaughter Chinese children, teens, and tots, in the name of feminism. I can imagine them stressing from age one; day one; stressing, like I can stress the perceived need for defense; stressing completely out, like preparing to die; falling unconscious like searching for an id; ID to show an enemy before EVERYONE inevitably gets murdered on a battlefield, including citizens' spouses. Fuck 'em all! They were already lucky enough to be loved at one point in their lives.

There's strength in numbers. So many Amériçaisians will need to get behind Japanese fighters. Fortunately, there will always be a Chinese citizen-fighter for every Japanese and Amériçaisian citizen-fighter. Perhaps no one will ever be outnumbered. Equal numbers of citizens on each side will be murdered in cold blood before global warming even sets in. To paraphrase Louis Fischer, Gandhi, and whoever Biblical figure came before them: if a heart is taken for every heart taken, there will be global pools of blood not being pumped around bodies. Maybe there will be a heart taken for every moment people take heart from.

Flags are the best. We have all been conditioned to fear red flags; socialism; China; danger; blood. Fortunately, to overcome such fear much blood must be spilled. This is exposure therapy. When citizens see the beauty of bloodshed, fighting for their life, and being in a warzone, they may eventually feel right at home, and want to now be doing so in such a place for many more great days, without fear. Perhaps the environment simply needs to be safe initially, like the ward I may presently be residing in. I'm not actually used to being in such a state as I am now. This doesn't excite me in the least. I'm almost fearful of this dreamy and dreary dead calmness. I just can't get used to this. I can only imagine being exposed to bloodshed to calm down.

Did I inadvertently save a baby? No. I don't want to think about that.

Warfare is the ultimate promotional campaign. Everything can be shown off to others, even if they refuse to see them point-blank, and ultimately get shot at point-blank range. Speaking of range, there is such an extensive range of weaponry to delight buyers the world over. It's wrong to not sell goods to citizens on the basis of their race. I want to see so many ethnically diverse people all gather so close to me before they all get murdered at once. There's no time for segregation. Everyone everywhere must die. The key is to bring people who hate one another as close to one another as possible, like they're protons in the sun and fusion is taking place. There must indeed be flare-ups of violence and disorder. There are enough weapons to go around the world. Warfare can go on tour.

'He looks so calm,' a woman says.

******

- Maroon 5 - Wake Up Call (Official Music Video)
https://youtu.be/dkQ0OJ5Byls

- The Weeknd - Call Out My Name (Official Video)
https://youtu.be/M4ZoCHID9GI

- The Economist
Asia | A wake-up call
War in Ukraine has bolstered Japan's support for a stronger army
https://www.economist.com/asia/2022/09/13/war-in-ukraine-has-bolstered-japans-support-for-a-stronger-army

- The House Committee on Veterans' Affairs
News / Press Releases

June 23, 2022

Chairman Takano Applauds House Passage of His Bipartisan Strong Veterans Act

The Strong Veterans Act will:

https://veterans.house.gov/news/press-releases/chairman-takano-applauds-house-passage-of-his-bipartisan-strong-veterans-act

["- Require explicit mental health and suicide prevention outreach to traditionally underserved veteran populations, including Native veterans"]

- Fox News

Abortion

Sen. Hirono blasted for 'call to arms' response to abortion bill: 'Sounds like she's calling for violence'

https://www.foxnews.com/media/sen-hirono-blasted-call-arms-response-abortion-bill-sounds-calling-violence

["Hawaii Democrat Sen. Mazie Hirono was criticized on Twitter for suggesting that it is time for a literal "call to arms" to fight against the pro-life movement."]

- Ed Markey

Senator Markey Joins Luján, Matsui, Colleagues in Introducing Legislation to Increase Digital Equity, Inclusion, and Literacy

https://www.markey.senate.gov/news/press-releases/senator-markey-joins-lujan-matsui-colleagues-in-introducing-legislation-to-increase-digital-equity-inclusion-and-literacy

- TH: Traditions Health

Blog

What Does a Coma Feel Like?

Dream-like State

Can Your Loved One Hear You?

https://www.traditionshealth.com/blog/what-does-a-coma-feel-like#:~:text=A%20coma%20is%20similar%20to,or%20communicate%20in%20any%20way.

["However, the brain may still be able to pick up on sounds from loved ones."]

- Medium
"An eye for an eye only ends up making the whole world blind."
https://medium.com/@steveagyeibeyondlifestyle/an-eye-for-an-eye-only-ends-up-making-the-whole-world-blind-a960ab767378

- Quote Investigator
An Eye for an Eye Will Make the Whole World Blind
Quote Investigator:
https://quoteinvestigator.com/2010/12/27/eye-for-eye-blind/
["...Louis Fischer, used a version of the expression when he wrote about Gandhi's approach to conflict. Fischer used the expression himself as part of his explanation of Gandhi's philosophy."]

- Book of Exodus (950 bce.)
[21:24: "Eye for eye, tooth for tooth."]

- PTSD Clinical Practice Guideline
PTSD: For Patients & Families
What Is Exposure Therapy?
https://www.apa.org/ptsd-guideline/patients-and-families/exposure-therapy
["The exposure to the feared objects, activities or situations in a safe environment helps reduce fear and decrease avoidance."]

- Energy Education
Nuclear fusion in the Sun
Figure 1.

https://energyeducation.ca/encyclopedia/
Nuclear_fusion_in_the_Sun

["Figure 1. The proton-proton fusion process that is the source of energy from the Sun. [1: a reference referred to in THIS source]"]

- Forbes

Science

A 'Dangerous' Sunspot with Major Solar Flare Potential Is Pointing at Earth

https://www.forbes.com/sites/ericmack/2022/09/01/a-dangerous-sunspot-with-major-solar-flare-potential-is-pointing-at-earth/

Chapter 9

Can I ever possibly be calm?

Perhaps if what I heard were hypersonic missiles covering the distance between Charlotte and Washington, D.C. in less than ten minutes, which powerful Aussies want to purchase, I could properly wake up. But all I heard was the voice of a woman; life on Earth; live.

I can't fly into the sky to look down on a mushroom cloud. I'm bedridden. I can't figuratively ride hypersonic missiles in order to not be overheard, when my every breath is now monitored. My mad thoughts may be free, but I have no way of turning them into the practice of harsh and hypersonic warfare, or the utterance of words to that effect. There's no sneaking up on anyone, figuratively or literally, when my SILENCE is just that: no time to talk. Growing dark realizations can hardly sneak up on legislators when I'm not liaising with enough of them to plant the associated seeds in their minds, like they're miniature hypersonic missiles to listen to in time.

I just want to PICK OUT the best MUSHROOMS when high in an atmosphere. I want to be the only one to see a magic mushroom in its entirety. No one CATCHES a fireball more than fifty seconds after citizens may become aware of a BLAST. Nuclear warfare can be an enjoyable game. Imagine a wave that has propagated through air all such time (even through gated communities), and for twelve miles, and now will propagate further through this medium at more than the standard sea level speed of sound. That's a missile that needn't even be material. Instead, an atom can simply be split.

The only unfortunate thing is that such intense fear is felt far too briefly. That being thought, I can't even give anyone a simple brief now, let alone influence them enough to convince them to endorse selling weapons to weird people, even just briefly.

There cannot be any real ACQUISITION while I'm out like a light. There are probably no mergers of military-industrial companies occurring. There is no gold about; no one buying gold if there were; no gold weaponry. No one is speaking my language of subtle and surreptitious warfare.

Considering just how many people can be maimed or killed by my weaponry, can be a joyous modus operandi, but now I have lost all hope of being near victims soon. And I want to simply be PRETENDING to be CLOSE to people, and not as close to and helpless by the side of kind nurses, as I presently am.

Hypersonic missiles can reach people hundreds of miles away in the space of a short break, before people finally break like storms. I don't need a break though. I could become too popular to push missiles without receiving backlash. Plus, I want to be working constantly on ways to take out poor strangers, without even breaking my stride. I have work to do. I need to be concentrating completely on the furtherance of suffering; the cleverness of MILITARY deception in everyday life, like war is in the air. If only I could be so smooth that the worst parts of any speech I give go in one ear and out the other of sheep, so fast that they're practically hypersonic missiles. Instant then constant suffering is a fine thought, when I'm not all alone in my thoughts; mindful of only myself, rather than the suffering of others. I want to be there, where they are, but not FOR them.

'Can we look into his eyes to see how conscious he is?' a woman asks. 'He may be furiously scanning the images of his dreams. We can try to understand what makes a hero tick.'

Like a bomb? Are my pupils moving like hypersonic missiles?

******

- Shaun Micallef's Mad as Hell
Series 15, Episode 9 (2022, September 14)
["Australia is considering acquiring hypersonic missiles capable of travelling between Melbourne and Sydney in just seven minutes." - Peter Mitchell / Newsreader for 7 News Melbourne]

- AtomicArchive.com
Science
> Effects of Nuclear Weapons
Overpressure
https://www.atomicarchive.com/science/effects/overpressure.html
["At 50 seconds after the explosion, when the fireball is no longer visible, the blast wave has traveled about 12 miles. It is then traveling at about 784 miles per hour, which is slightly faster than the speed of sound at sea level."]

- Frontiers
Frontiers in Psychology, 31 October 2018
Section Theoretical and Philosophical Psychology
Rapid Eye Movements in Sleep Furnish a Unique Probe into Consciousness
https://www.frontiersin.org/articles/10.3389/fpsyg.2018.02087/full
["...REMs during sleep may index an internalized active sampling or 'scanning' of self-generated visual constructs..."]

- Dr. Strangelove (1964)
[On the associated poster, a man is riding a nuclear bomb.]

Chapter 10

It would seem as though there is universal approval of private citizens' universal cooperation with the military-industrial complex and Amériçaisian Department of Defense, given how universities accept dirty money from these bodies. Students are effectively taught to love and admire MICDoD like it's McDonald's. Much research conducted by Australians and Amériçaisians at certain universities is funded by governments in open cahoots with the Australian Department of Defence; cooperating with the Australian Department of Defence. In the space of almost six years, this body gave fifteen public universities a collective sum of twenty-one-million Australian dollars. The associated government planned and plans to allocate two-hundred-and-seventy-billion such dollars to defense over the decade that began at the tail end of yesteryear. Strong nationalistic TIES are totally fashionable.

Things should and must be going as I've already planned before becoming comatose, but now I feel like I'm simply lying comatose and watching the world go by, with no agency. Some AGENCY is always necessary and crucial. There can be no life without it, and hopefully none WITH it too, though I personally want to survive; to be like the mastermind behind Squid Game, but forever in the shadows I doubt I'm in now. A real-life Squid Game is any given psychopath's MILITARY dream. Weaponry must be remarkable and utilized perfectly. Bonds must be close and then ruthlessly severed. People often drop the ball on objectives. They get killed and become mere objects; loose marbles. But I'm a VIP. It just bothers me that I'm presently perpetually comatose.

I can't even hear any lines now, like I'm not on any set. I'm in my own silent bubble that could even be deemed intellectual. I don't know if those around me have fallen silent, or if such silence is purely personal and mental. This is in stark contrast to the sounds of agonized warfare. I just want to pay someone to take me to where carnage is taking place so that I can subsequently revel in its aftermath. But any movement is impossible. Some effective MOVEMENT is so unbelievable that it may as well be a pacific one; one for peace.

My life is limited to following personal trains of thought, and figuratively shifting gears or changing tracks when appropriate. How did I get here? A bomb must have gone off in Franklin Park. I was thusly rendered comatose. My ears now ring almost like they're BURNING. This may last for sixteen hours to two days, or from one-hundred-and-sixty-eight hours to three-hundred-and-thirty-six hours if I'm not lucky. But I usually am, present comatose state aside.

I'm sure that these people around me don't think that I need to be educated, other than physically perhaps. Do I have a leg to stand on? Will I stand OUT in a crowd? These people probably think of me more as a scholar of the highest order. And that's logical, given many scholars receive cash from bodies for defense, and Queen Elizabeth the second was presumably an educator of the highest order, or at least granted high orders to others, and poor people in Kenya were tortured and put in concentration camps when they were seeking independence while under the reign of this monarch that ultimately lasted almost three quarters of a century. It's unfortunate that such people were not tortured for just as long. What the governmental body of her country did, she could have stopped. Likewise, I could stop weaponry flooding into distant lands, but I choose not to. Before Kenyan independence, many of the Kikuyu people in remote areas, villages, and British gulags, were killed, fucked without their consent, forced to work, tortured, and/or got sick and/or starved. Yet we all hail the mighty monarch, whoever that figurehead may be. I can rest assured that I am being equally admired at present despite being a psychopathic mastermind. Further, I hold a PhD in international relations, so I am officially a doctor. I've been trying to make it safely to my figurative surgery to oversee carnage up close. Many would close up about such affairs. But I absolutely love death, carnage, and royalty. Killing people without suffering any consequences is incredibly simple when some status is high enough. The Queen was even given greater personal sovereign immunity than that which was traditional. She could already avoid prosecution and having to answer for shady actions, but this just wasn't enough for this powerful monarch. Essentially, the only prosecution that was and is allowed is warfare where poor people are the victims.

Basically, violence is worth paying good money for, and the best and brightest minds agree. Death is an appropriate price to pay for rebellion of sorts. We all idolize warmongers in all shapes and sizes. That's what identity politics is all about: the appropriate marketing of warfare. The colors must be just right, and the full red of blood not put on display to the general however-accommodating public. Identity politics is the creation of a closed door that lobbyists like me can operate behind as free evil spirits who are independent enough to figuratively occupy the minds of ordinary people without them even being privy to this. Killing is fine when done in the name of the finest powerful people. To follow a traditional course means to perpetually condone anachronistic warfare. Every associated COURSE must not be changed. Collision courses are desirable, like the breaking down of peace talks. To become a successful psychopath requires years of study at a prestigious university. Flying under the radar requires the expertise to use any RADAR without remorse; mental ingenuity and physical skills. As little attention is paid to a qualified psychopath as they themselves pay to the needs of their victims. Everything must be perfectly off the radar. Focus must be paramount and mastered. Apathy is also a key to a successful and meaningful kill. Eventually the brazenness of an act is diluted by its permissibility, so that formerly brazen yet formal act after such act can be committed in the manner of a brazen unashamed homicide addict. A formal education is necessary for this. Formally, such an act is like a ceremonial ballet. Warfare is formally sanctioned like poor countries.

'This is AOC,' a woman says.

Is AOC here?

'You're a hero, Hill,' AOC continues. 'You saved a baby.'

I did what?! What a magnificent ceremonial ballet.

I suppose that appreciating some national INDUSTRY is something to work toward, perhaps through engaging in warfare. That's hard work. Presently BODIES are a shadow of what they possibly can be. They can be admired the world over; COUNTED. Amériçaisian casualties in Iraq were mostly under the age of thirty. That counts for something. They died so beautifully young. I know that I'm figuratively ON THE RIGHT TRACK when thusly WALKING ON THE SHOULDERS of members of supposedly progressive parties. I then run serious and immoral errands better than any despot I know.

Working under people is effortful. Doing it well, so that some REALM remains just as it should, is paramount. No one should change the subjects studied. Students should stay focused on the need for warfare. Universities are kingdoms are ruled by necessary capitalists. And I'm a necessary psychopathic tool; a spanner in the working man; a needle in the eyes of stacks of objectified innocent civilians; a thorn in the backsides of future bodies; generations; a global winner. This can all be expertly objectified in prose. My prime moves make me look like the object of my desire: a cybernetic organism, to spell it out properly. Emotion is for human retards, unless it's purely and constantly sadistic glee.

Perhaps I move a single finger.

But no one says anything that I can hear.

******

- Black Agenda Report

Decolonizing the Mind

https://www.blackagendareport.com/decolonizing-mind

["Elizabeth bore responsibility for every UK government action during her 70-year long reign. The concentration camps and torture in Kenya during the independence struggle were her responsibility.";

"Decolonized people know that the prestigious universities they are told to admire receive funds from the Defense Department and the military industrial complex."]

- Honi Soit.

Analysis

Universities are deeply embedded in Australia's military buildup

https://honisoit.com/2021/11/universities-are-deeply-embedded-in-australias-military-buildup/

["The existence of federally-funded research collaborations between Australia and the US is a grave concern."]

["...the government committing $270 billion on defence spending in the next decade...";

"...since 2016, the Department of Defence has provided nearly $21 million in funding across 15 public universities."]

- Squid Game (2021)

Season 1

9. One Lucky Day

["The game's creator steps out of the shadows."]

- Squid Game (2021)

Season 1

7. VIPS

[The VIPs pay good money to view scenes of carnage.]

- Squid Game (2021)
Season 1
6. Gganbu
[The pivotal conversation between Kang Sae-byeok and Ji-yeong, followed by the dropping of the marble, is remarkable.]

- Squid Game (2021)
Season 1

- Healthline
How to Stop and Prevent Your Ears from Ringing After a Concert
How long does the ringing last?
https://www.healthline.com/health/ears-ringing-after-concert#_noHeaderPrefixedContent
["Occasional exposure to loud noise can bring about temporary tinnitus.";
"These symptoms often go away within 16 to 48 hours. In extreme cases, it may take a week or two."]

- The Guardian
Uncovering the brutal truth about the British empire
https://www.theguardian.com/news/2016/aug/18/uncovering-truth-british-empire-caroline-elkins-mau-mau
["This system – "Britain's gulag", as Elkins called it – had affected far more people than previously understood.";
"In camps, villages and other outposts, the Kikuyu suffered forced labour, disease, starvation, torture, rape and murder."]

- The Guardian
Queen's consent investigations
Revealed: Queen's sweeping immunity from more than 160 laws
Strengthening protection
https://www.theguardian.com/uk-news/2022/jul/14/queen-immunity-british-laws-private-property

["...why has it been necessary for so many personal exemptions to be written into law, when the monarch is already immune to prosecution or civil action by virtue of the centuries-old doctrine of sovereign immunity?"]

- MTV

Life

Almost 70 Percent of U.S. Casualties in Iraq Under Age 30

https://www.mtv.com/news/d5706i/almost-70-percent-of-us-casualties-in-iraq-under-age-30

Chapter 11: Hear #1

TRIGGER WARNING

I can't see the faces of the people hovering over me, but I imagine they can see mine; my face with my innermost thoughts shining through. I want to look agreeable, like I'm a person being forced to bury some dead or BE dead. I feel like I've somehow lost consciousness after shoving people under a literal bulldozer like a bus, like they're bodies, as a homicidal virgin. I feel like I've found this more pleasurable than nauseating. All the while, feeling personal pity is improbable, like comprehension and free will. I'm STUPORedly catatonic, permanently figuratively up, and refraining from drinking and eating in order to better appreciate and sense the sick atmosphere of death and decay.

Maybe some woman's gazing into my deceptively gentle eyes.

'You've been seeing me so regularly that I think you may have a problem,' a female optometrist says.

Is she talking to me?

That's WHY I'm seeing you, if I even am. You keep telling me that I have a problem.

I feel like I grab her and pull her so close to me that she's hurting horribly.

'I can't keep seeing you,' this woman says.

I'm so SICK but maybe I'm just fleshing thoughts out next to bodies being fleshed. Have I been fleshed to be so hungry? Whom can I now flesh with atrocities?

I want to listen to her scream, intently.

'Ahhhhh,' the woman cries.

Maybe I'm having an autonomous sensory meridian response in my upper to lower body now, almost like I'm a herorin[e] addict.

I want to be the six feet of ground suffocating her.

'What are you doing!?' this woman of my dreams shrieks into my organ of Corti.

Maybe I've exposed my true self to her now.

I dig my nails deep into her back like that's a coffin, to hear those fine high notes that punctuate every known emotional melody.

'Eiiiiiii,' this woman cries.

That pitch is perfect; reflecting perfect pain.

I want her to nod in agreement that ARMS are necessary for wistful abandonment preceding satisfaction, so I place my hands snugly around her supple neck like they're a brace for it! Brace for it! Screaming echoes are sensual. Asphyxiation occurs. I maybe move my arms up and down.

She gasps.

Fight me! Try to fight me, feminist! Strike at me, Israeli soldier. Let me use your strength against you. Fuck consent because we're at war. She will nod to death; off to death.

I throw her body without letting it go. I toss it one way then another like she's a joystick. I control more than merely her. Women now come at me from every which direction, like trying to gently coddle me, but I cobble together such figures as methodically as a mathematician. I take them all on to bury them alive; bury them like I've always buried overt displays of psychopathic thrill; like these females always bury themselves in humanitarian work. I'm hardly burying my face in ARMS in shame. I cobble together every bit of pollution I can get my grubby hands on in order to prepare to bury such beings.

It excites me when they hit the low notes en masse as they fall on top of one another, and just before they cry out for the last time. I force forty females I sequentially face. Reactions are both opposite and equal. Cries are the best forces of exhalation; forced voices, as forces in nursing join forces to take me on; in. However, this heavy nursery of nurses cannot now RISE UP in any revolt against me. They cannot be raised from the dead as easily as ra[is/z]ing a BLOCK to their swollen, sultry, and sullen black lips and eyes. Reactions can never be old, like victims. All I can hear is ever newer confirmation of pain, like of a judge that's only ever me.

I can't for the life of me figure out where all these women are coming from.

Some screams sound like they're of joy. This confuses me immensely.

The women and their screams arrest me, like they're officers, but it's hard to arrest the horrors of the obscene situation that's afoot. My thoughts and prayers go to myself, and I believe that I'm independently and solely deep in them. I cannot see beyond the globe of my cranium, but I hear that all women want is outer space. My hearing is becoming ever less numb. The women may now be numb, like numbness was contagious just now. Maybe they're now callous, calculating, and cold.

Sharp cries tend not to match the mental images of motionless mouths figuratively before me. This lack of synchronicity is disturbing. I may truly have no idea what's really going on. A comprehensive account of this would ultimately require comprehension. A world of happenings could be unfolding before my very eyelids, but it's a REFLECTION on certain PUPILS that women are even more lost; that all people can't study. I can't begin to truly comprehend some traditional REFLECTION. I stand out.

I don't GET sleep that's deep. That's OUT OF MY DEPTH. And maybe out of the depth of my drive that's generally remarkable. Instead, I'm not fit to even so much as genuinely eat or drink my senses silly. All I can do at present is listen intently to the raspy and nervous exhalations of fearful women by my 'drums. They're perhaps too scared to say anything substantial. I can't really know, or generously PLACE A SINGLE FINGER ON, what's left of them to talk about; just why they're silent. There are so few PARTS for them that they're like BACKGROUND in a war film. Perhaps they're objects if not extras. Do they even have limbs? That's maybe MY kind of BACKGROUND. I can't remember. What are the scenes I love most of my true past?

'Hill!' a woman yells.

I want her to be in agony so I wouldn't answer even if I could.

'Hill!' she yells again, her voice raspy like that of a professional autonomous sensory meridian responser.

I kind of want to keep hearing her voice, like I don't mind going to sleep. Or do I prefer crying? I may grind my teeth to the beat of women's exhalations when trying to rack my brain or said women. I may bite my nails when thinking that they're not mine.

Keep calling my name.

******

- The Weeknd - Call Out My Name (Official Video)
https://youtu.be/M4ZoCHID9GI

- "I Buried Thousands in Secret Mass Graves" | Informer
https://youtu.be/lmmsLJhrmPE
["I couldn't say no. If they saw on my face that I didn't agree with them, they would put me with them [the dead people]." - Syrian Bulldozer Driver / Informer;

"...and then he told me to push the bodies down with the bulldozer. The first time I did it, I passed out." - Syrian Bulldozer Driver / Informer;

"All the time I was doing this work, my brain wasn't working. It stopped comprehending. It stopped feeling." - Syrian Bulldozer Driver / Informer;

"We couldn't eat, drink, sleep at night." - Syrian Bulldozer Driver / Informer]

- Sam Harris - Free Will
https://youtu.be/iA6Qc8h8ulQ
[The quote is from Free Will (2012).]

- The Times of Israel
IDF expands combat roles for women, but says most are not cut out for elite units
https://www.timesofisrael.com/idf-expands-combat-roles-for-women-but-says-most-not-cut-out-for-elite-units/

- The American Journal of Forensic Medicine and Pathology
Autoerotic Asphyxiation in a Female
https://journals.lww.com/amjforensicmedicine/Abstract/2000/
06000/Autoerotic_Asphyxiation_in_a_Female.4.aspx

- The Physics Classroom
Physics Tutorial » Newton's Laws
Newton's Laws - Lesson 4 - Newton's Third Law of Motion
Newton's Third Law
For every action, there is an equal and opposite reaction.
https://www.physicsclassroom.com/class/newtlaws/Lesson-4/
Newton-s-Third-Law

- Healthline
How Much Deep, Light, and REM Sleep Do You Need?
https://www.healthline.com/health/how-much-deep-sleep-do-you-
need

- Sleep Foundation
How Noise Can Affect Your Sleep Satisfaction
What is ASMR and How Can It Help You Sleep?
https://www.sleepfoundation.org/noise-and-sleep/asmr#:

- The Conversation
ASMR is linked to anxiety and neuroticism, our new research finds
https://theconversation.com/asmr-is-linked-to-anxiety-and-
neuroticism-our-new-research-finds-175903

Chapter 12: Hear #2

'Do we hit the button associated with life support?' a female nurse asks.

I can't see where she's going with this.

I can't even begin to imagine personal, global, and mental annihilation that's almost like an inner nuclear war. If they simply press a button, will I die? Liz Truss would probably press it. She's willing, ready, and a dutiful sheep. But I can bring her arms galore. I'm not sure if any important button is the best thing to press right now. I'm somewhat nausea'd out as nausea blankets me; me who once had blanket authority to remove any blankets from my body at the very least. I've been indirectly applauded for supplying people with arms used to maim many more; the demise of the very keen clappers themselves.

Some time ago, the tradition of communicating global information on arms changing hands and money spent on them, was broken with. The Amériçaisian State Department felt that fifty annual versions of an associated report were enough, and quietly resolved to stop publishing them, as mentioned somewhere on a minor page of the latest National Defense Authorization Act. Meanwhile, arms sent from Amériçaisia to Ukraine could end up in anyone's hands because Amériçaisians can't keep an eye on them; track them to appropriate locations. Also, people change track now and then, and become traitors. Arms may or may not be used to kill a leader; ANY leader.

Security for Ukraine may have been costing Amériçaisians one-hundred-million dollars daily for over a year so far. Without public question, the calls for excessive associated funding are readily answered, and peaceful diplomacy is forgotten. The war is forever ongoing, and

I need to live to see more people die. People like Lindsey German highlight how powerful Brits are pushing arms to Ukrainians, and talking tough. Such peaceniks want this to stop. I don't. I'm just sad that so many people are dying while my eyes are closed.

I need to open my eyes, like the world does.

'Does he need support?' another nurse asks.

Everyone needs arms. But if they're going to press one particular button then I want to chop their fingers off one by one; bite their digits off their supple hands. That button is not a chew-toy. DOGS shouldn't even mull the figurative mulling of certain buttons over.

These nurses are already pushing my buttons. I like WEAPONS that are effective, sure, but this particular banter to provoke me into talking, is not my cup of tea. If only I could be guaranteed a seat on a spacecraft before nuclear bombs are dropped the world over, I would be content. But merely having a birds-eye view of people who have been exposed to nuclear fallout, rather than coming face to face with them, is less than ideal. And if I'm in outer space then how can I have enough tickets on myself if too few people can reach me to put them on me? I need people to be cold enough to want to get then stay in touch with me, then to watch them suffocate before my universal eyes, as the entire world suffers in the background. A backdrop of global suffering is key to magnificence. Rounds of applause should echo the usage of rounds of arms. That's figuratively thinking smaller and smaller almost to the point of figuratively splitting the atom. Then I can willfully and gleefully think ahead.

'We have no way to tell what he's thinking,' a nurse says.

That's right. My thoughts are like revelations about expenditure on arms: not for public minds. Psychopathy is far easier when genocidal thoughts escape the mere prospect of verbal utterance rather than my lips. I can imagine I'm like a black and blank slate they can only ever forever polish feverishly. My mind has been figuratively redacted. They can only watch ONE line: the depiction of the electrical activity of my heart over periods. Since I'm heartless, they're looking at nothing much. I can imagine silencing them so much that they feel like me but far more tortured by doubt and fearful as they contemplate their fragile existence. I can imagine banging heads together rather than merely hands in order to MAKE THE same NOISE. People notice savage beatings. They pay avid attention to cranial bloodshed and like the concept of PICKING BRAINS. Which intelligent peaceniks should be picked first? Put all their heads together. With no oversight, brutality can mimic that of even more than merely fifty years ago before certain expenditures on arms were made public, presumably.

I want to watch people puke at the prospect of having millions of innocent lives in their butterfingers. Things are dropped like balls. They move like vomit falls over lips. Powerful people should merely bark out bombastic and incendiary demands while puking and panicking. Only the sea should be calm, when bodies have sunk to the ocean floor. Quotas of casualties have already been signed for; picked. Happenings have been set in stone and balls are rolling, like heads in both instances. If only I could get out of mine in order to take my front-row seat to carnage.

'I'll see if we can get him to open his eyes,' a woman whispers into my ear.

Her hushed voice is remarkable in its frequency. The traffic of sound waves through my ear canal is super smooth, almost like tear gas being sprayed around protesters. The sensation is admittedly rather incredible and exciting.

Ok. I'll listen to what you have to say.

'Wake up, Hill,' the woman pleads. 'The world is your oyster.'

That's rather soft like her sensual voice.

This autonomous sensory meridian responser is exceptional and talented. My sense of sound is being newly awakened, like citizens awaken to atrocities. I'm perplexed, to say the least. But she says more.

'We're here for you,' the woman continues. 'We'll be by your side until and after you emerge from your coma. We want to cordially welcome you back into a fully conscious state, when you're ready and willing. We want to bring you into this world afresh.'

******

- The Pussycat Dolls - Buttons (Official Music Video) ft. Snoop Dogg
https://youtu.be/VCLxJd1d84s

- You Couldn't Make This Sh*t Up
https://youtu.be/wo1xha9GTEE
["...will you press the old button?" - Russell Brand / Political Commentator;

"It would mean global annihilation." - John Pienaar / Times Radio Host;

"I won't ask you would you press the button. You will say yes. But faced with that task I would feel physically sick." - John Pienaar / Times Radio Host;

"I think it's an important duty of the Prime Minister. I'm ready to do that." - Liz Truss / British Prime Minister;

"That's literally an audience of people applauding their own demise." - Russell Brand / Political Commentator]

- LET: Law Enforcement Today

"Most transparent administration in history" stops publishing military expenditures, arms transfers report

https://www.lawenforcementtoday.com/biden-stops-publishing-military-expenditures-arms-transfers-report/

["This week, the State Department announced that the World Military Expenditures and Arms Transfers report, which has been published for over 50 years, will no longer be produced. As usual, that provision was buried deep inside the National Defense Authorization Act for FY 2022..."];

"The elimination of this important program comes as sources say that the United States is virtually unable to track what happens to the military equipment and weapons being sent to Ukraine ostensibly to fight against Vladimir Putin's invading Russian army."]

- The Intercept_

U.S. Military Aid to Ukraine Grows to Historic Proportions — Along with Risks

https://theintercept.com/2022/09/10/ukraine-military-aid-weapons-oversight/

["...some analysts estimate the true figure of the U.S. commitment to Ukraine is much higher: up to $40 billion in security assistance, or $110 million a day over the last year.";

"The relentless stream of funding announcements, in the absence of any public discussion of what the U.S. is doing to seek an end to the conflict, has signaled to critics a recognition that there is no end in sight to the war, and that the U.S. is committed to supporting Ukrainian defense efforts for the long haul rather than pursue a negotiated end to it."]

- Common Dreams

Boris Johnson Pressured Zelenskyy to Ditch Peace Talks with Russia: Ukrainian Paper

https://www.commondreams.org/news/2022/05/06/boris-johnson-pressured-zelenskyy-ditch-peace-talks-russia-ukrainian-paper

[""The British government has become an obstacle to peace in Ukraine by encouraging the continuation of the war through huge arms shipments and incendiary rhetoric," Lindsey German, convenor of the U.K.-based Stop the War Coalition, said in a statement..."]

- Financial Review
Ukraine calls for more Western arms after Russian setback
https://www.afr.com/world/europe/ukraine-calls-for-more-western-arms-after-russian-setback-20220913-p5bhrj

- Sleep Foundation
How Noise Can Affect Your Sleep Satisfaction
What is ASMR and How Can It Help You Sleep?
https://www.sleepfoundation.org/noise-and-sleep/asmr

Chapter 13: Feel #1

The abrasions on my skin against something like the surface of a T-NinetyM tank from Russia that there has possibly been little abrasion of, excites and alarms me in equal measure. Metal is being used to cut such skin. I need to leave my body. Maybe it's touch-and-go whether a pilot is attempting touch-and-goes on my personal terrain? I can't know. I EVER(-)wonder (as I, by definition, typically do; always do now, and more and more often) if this is so.

I feel weird.

The abrasive penetration of metal into my skin, perhaps accompanying the abrasive undertakings of a surgeon or forensic pathologist, may profoundly affect me completely, though I'm at a loss as to whether this is satisfying like piercing boiling water I somehow can't hear running over itchy skin; that I can imagine as menacingly piercing dark eyes. Some personal shell could be thusly pierced. I want to be in charge here. But I can't scream and so screams cannot be accordingly piercing, whether mine or eventually those of those surrounding me like tanks. My analysis of happenings cannot be piercing enough, but my questions can be. And I only have questions. That's maybe fine, since I just have time to think for my true self, and I privately violently dislike company I want to pierce in precisely the ways that were previously alluded to. Abhorrent and indiscriminate vengeance is more than skin-deep. It's heartless.

I only want to explore the interior of an inanimate tank from Russia; to find the latest tech like shopping about for an iPhone; to find the greatest inanimate model on Earth, like it's an animate Russian one.

This could be an educational experience for armies, I, and the rest of the West.

Someone maybe has a dig at me while giving me a dig in the abdomen by digging a scalpel of sorts deep into it. I could be done for. I can't move but the section of me this person's dividing into two is moved against my will; to be REmoved from me perhaps, like my life is still to be continued.

Perhaps loaded guns, tanks, and rich and drunk people are around me. TANKS can certainly be LOADED, like such terms, given certain actions. Fearfulness is as fundamental as rights and wrongs. People can be drunk on power; eager to learn about life and death from psychopathic superiors. Others can be frozen in fear. Vehicles can be as still as chambers as tanks as cells as people on deathbeds of bedrock. That's the bedrock of an orgy that's the bedrock of my dreams. Bodies can be cut in half like butter so that what extras are inside can be spread out on surfaces like microchips. Metal is so useful exponentially. People can figuratively COVER CIRCUITS of MACROchips. But they will be captured and tortured for the sake of educating people about the thrill of electronic warfare.

My range of sensual, fleshly, and worldly desires is limited by my inability to see, taste and smell anything associated with a single spell of autonomous activity. I have no significant spell at present. However, my sensory range may be limited, but my creative range isn't too bad. I can still easily think about what I want done to people in my name or Waytheon's. There is little amiss about my intent to kill or have people killed. Top individuals like myself essentially casually order the murders of ever greater numbers of civilians, tops, as their riches top ever greater bucks. Simple people see tops. Tanks are too heavy to wear, but they're put on display on (top of) bodies on battlefields like catwalks. Ordinary civilians not at the top must only see tops; not be told the truth concerning the dire need for COVERS that must not get

BLOWN like tires; must forever look up at/to stars; war heroes; top guns.

Lately, I've been feeling; at least hearing, and feeling things against my skin. That's two senses covered. I'm supremely confident that I will come to ALL my senses soon. The latest that someone can hear and feel is certainly the ground below them rumbling violently. Having a sense of being powerful while sensing others' trepidation, as I yearn to, is fashionable beyond associated words. Touching on this is so essential. The latest significant speech is surely a plutocrat's.

People can be LATE. The penalty for not being punctual can be death. I like to think about civilians thinking about their LATE friends; spouses. The latter may have broken up with soldiers or vice versa. Some are surely under tanks as surely as they were once under the weather. They were not just physically exhausted, but emotionally also. A simple touch may be all it takes to kill a straggler. That's the thrill of powerful powerful warfare that's very great.

The brush of one woman's skin against mine may EFFECTIVELY INTIMATELY affect me truthfully and successfully, though without sight and other senses I can't quite go into intimate detail in order to verify this. Is this sensation affecting me well, privately, and well-privately sexually? I affect curiosity.

I think I'm feeling a little better now.

******

- Justin Timberlake - Rock Your Body (Official Video)
https://youtu.be/TSVHoHyErBQ

- The Economist
The Economist explains

Why the capture of a Russian T-90M tank matters

https://www.economist.com/the-economist-explains/2022/09/26/why-the-capture-of-a-russian-t-90m-tank-matters

["The top-of-the-range model is loaded with the latest tech. Western armies can learn from it"]

Chapter 14: Feel #2

I want to direct this presumably pathological medical cartel around me, to the side of some disparate and pathetic lost soul, like they're elite members of the Jalisco New Generation Cartel in Mexico. Their violence and brutality have been unmatched by any prospective peers, since the cartel's inception. Members of other such gangs have nothing on them. They have and proudly flash visible sniper rifles that are fifty caliber, machine guns that are heavy, grenade launchers, and assault rifles that the launchers are on the barrels of, about. They also have rocket-propelled grenades that can and have been used to destroy helicopters of the national and traditional armed forces, tanks made by hand and man and dubbed Los Monstruos, and drones for exterminating cartels against them and security services. They're probably enough arms. I can now feel my own and I long to FEEL ever more.

It always strikes me that civilians can easily be struck with intense fear when arms are great enough. Further, infections can strike at any time and soldiers from wherever will strike again and again. Gangrenous arms can fall off lost souls[,] because they're DEAD WEIGHTS. Blood can be going everywhere but through legs and arms, but bacteria can be figuratively picking up the slack; where blood was; giving new life to bodies.

GRAPHIC accounts of widespread profiteering through warfare paint a holy and bleak picture that no one merely mortal human can paint better. Accounts get done beautifully. The hope of victims who are ill at ease is lost. Aspiring artists suffer to death. The wheels never stop turning on annihilation. The wheels are los monstruos. Associated imagery is epic; profound. Signs are like Hollywood's; like lightning;

like the weapons as sharp as ingrown hairs; as well-audible cracks; as tongues; as disappointment; as ingrown military worlds; as civilians' own such ingrown worlds; as movements; as understandable and clear support for warfare; as an image that's a thousand callous words; as cries; as ears and eyes of fearful people; as pain; as blows; as bitter tastes left in mouths; as evil desires; as reminders of imminent doom; as enemies with one another; as true psychopaths; as weak and nervous inhalations; as undeniable fear; as a rapid elevation of blood pressure; as hands around necks; and as violent habits performed artfully well. Many people know what they're up against. Many people willfully put themselves in harm's way. I love that. And I absolutely love when they regret it when it's remarkably too late.

RUBBING arms IN civilians' FACES is a means of controlling them to the teeth while armed to such teeth. If there will be blood on bodies, soldiers should rub it in. I would gloat and smile if I were afforded some last chances to perform mannerisms, like to speak with actions rather than words. Civilians can be packed like sardines in an obscenely horrific scenario.

Contact can be completely human; made by women with myself, like tanks might be. Maybe women can fly down to meet me, like angels, in choppers that have been shot down using RPGs, and now beg for mercy by my side. CHOPPERS can be moved by psychopaths; held like axes; and parts of bodies can be used to clean them like they're the teeth of cannibals. Being truly armed to the teeth is totally imaginable. CHOPPERS can truly be too close for comfort, and it can be all hands on deck making sure that blades are properly used. Lost victims can barely even PUT THEIR FINGERS ON ANYTHING. DRONES can be terrifying enough to send shivers down spines. This SOUND[']S as bad as it is. Blades can be touching the blades of tongues. Nothing should COVER BLADES except for telemarketers. Things will ultimately be TASTELESS. Just picking up certain blades can draw blood, but I wonder what can be drawn on me.

A nurse draws circles on my skin with a fingertip, then I feel the undulating contours of a soft SKIN'Y bulb against my chest, that's tight like a garment, members of vicious armed forces, or shady security, but unlike my chest. I think that maybe I'm not anxious, injured, and nor do I have a chest infection. I can begin to breathe better. This nurse is drawing on me like I'm a canvas. Could my hairs be standing on end like fine lines of black ink?

She draws ever larger circles, like trying to ensure that my entire chest will soon be surrounded by a single tip being moved sensually and slowly along the soft surface just above my cutaneous nerves.

The motion of her tip intrigues me no end. This is a surprisingly spine-tingling action.

Can I be struck on a nurse looking after me?; struck by her beauty? Will I ever see great arms enough?; see every pore? It occurs to me that several people here are perhaps in no fearful hurry nor fearful. They're touching my skin like trying to figure out whether there's an infection in any part of me. They touch me carefully again and again, and move fingers of hands down like not surrendering.

Some fight continues, and maybe for survival. What could be in me that's being put up? I think. This is HARD.

******

- Robbie Williams - Feel (Official Video)
https://youtu.be/iy4mXZN1Zzk

- Mariah Carey - Touch My Body (Official Music Video)
https://youtu.be/9b8erWuBA44

- Mexico's Most Wanted Drug Kingpin | The War on Drugs
https://youtu.be/2RZoGOc3VCs
["Since they formed, the CJNG's calling card has very simply been to make themselves the most brutal and violent cartel around." - Jamie Clifton / VICE Reporter and Writer;

"They're armed with assault rifles, with grenade launches attached to the barrel, heavy machine guns, and also this gun. This is a .50 caliber sniper rifle. It's a powerful weapon that the CJNG loves to show off." - Jamie Clifton / VICE Reporter and Writer;

"They have what they call Los Monstruo[s], which are really basically handmade man-made tanks..." - Luis Chaparro / Journalist;

"...the CJNG used RPGs to shoot down a military helicopter..." - Jamie Clifton / VICE Reporter and Writer;

"Meanwhile, the CJNG have also pioneered the use of weaponized drones to attack both the security services and rival cartels." - Jamie Clifton / VICE Reporter and Writer]

- NCBI: National Center for Biotechnology Information; NLM: National Library of Medicine; NIH: National Institute of Health
PMC: PubMed Central®
Epidemiology and Infection
Microbiology and risk factors associated with war-related wound infections in the Middle East
https://www.ncbi.nlm.nih.gov/pmc/articles/PMC9150393/#

- Common Dreams
Weeks After Biden Fist-Bumps Saudi Prince, US OKs $5 Billion in Gulf Arms Deals
https://www.commondreams.org/news/2022/08/02/weeks-after-biden-fist-bumps-saudi-prince-us-oks-5-billion-gulf-arms-deals

- Mayo Clinic
Patient Care & Health Information > Diseases & Conditions
Gangrene

Overview

https://www.mayoclinic.org/diseases-conditions/gangrene/
symptoms-causes/syc-20352567

["Gangrene is death of body tissue due to a lack of blood flow or a serious bacterial infection. Gangrene commonly affects the arms and legs..."]

- Healthline
Why Does My Chest Feel Tight?
https://www.healthline.com/health/tight-chest
["Reasons include infection, injury, anxiety..."]

Chapter 15: Taste #1

Something is touched to my tongue.

Thought pales in comparison to sensation. All I need to do now is keep my mouth open; almost pretend to be diplomatic, like Washington, while thoughtlessly acting utterly dependently like an ideologue; Liz Truss. I can't do much now either. Whatever's done TO ME could be at the whim of the West's top managers. Thoughtless righteousness unites Américaisians. Righteous thoughtlessness unites Brits. Reckless conservatism against all changing odds requires dogged determination. Now, I personally can perhaps only be sensible figuratively; insofar as sensing sourness. Being rational may be overrated anyway. I can relate to so many aggressive warmongers even more nowahours. Biden could be by my side tasting an Américaisian apple pie. I'm as proud of Biden as I am of the last leader to lead civilians into war; EVERY LAST leader leading civilians into war. In the state I'm in now, I am almost sitting back and watching critically criminal affairs unfold while hardly thinking critically at all; with a temperament that's hardly critical at all; while surely still critically successful. My condition is as CRITICAL as key happenings that precede change; important, and I could just DIE. Is my body becoming hard like decisions made ever more foolishly nowadays? When things are running smoothly for victorious warmongers, thought is unnecessary. To perhaps draw nearer to Biden, I try to be stale and get stuck in the past like it's somehow stimulation of nerves or unnecessary global revolutions, to get stuck into; like into some Américaisian apple pie. I need to be thoughtless in order to taste his sweet apple pie. Forget about thinking this through.

The taste of some flake is so sharp that I feel as though a great cry of unconditional triumph is coming from the back of my throat.

Mindless sweet talk is hardly even necessary anymore. I want something SUBSTANTIAL. Sweetness and diplomacy don't fill me with joy, like sweets don't fill me up. I taste something bitter that reminds me of me when I've been powerless, and how I maybe am; of sorry and pathetic civilians putting their lives on the line for land alone. SOURNESS reminds me of acid attacks not wholly divorced from bombing. Sour looks of victims of warfare inevitably get overlooked as salt gets rubbed into wounds. I taste the salt of tears; salt of victims. I taste something like monosodium glutamate; umami. My tongue becomes strikingly hot then cold. Am I still cool and hot? I think I taste chilis then gelato.

I think about food I can't consume. I guess it would therefore be sensible to be utterly thoughtless like starving and desperate civilians before and after wars; like warmongers behind such wars. Numbness precedes the reckless slashing of limbs; the figurative stepping back while jamming knives into the hearts of lost souls. I feel more numb than what victims can possibly feel, and I feel great about that. It's like no one can touch me and nothing affects me. But there's surely something on my tongue. Tongues can be less sharp than the taste of blood. How many such tongues can cushion a blow? Fearful civilians bite tongues. Can I see gueules cassées? Blows to the face are common in modern warfare, as four in ten terribly wounded soldiers who fought in Afghanistan and Iraq have/had facial wounds. Blanket pushing on is like pushing a blanket onto me. I taste some FABRIC, like something's caving in on me. But I won't just rise from ashes. I'll wear them like they're female psychopaths' glass ceilings.

TASTES are becoming unusually bitter for my liking. But can I soon cast BITTER judgements to my taste, while peaceniks get angry, and focus only on pain?

I'm experienced at turning blind eyes to change, but now I can't even as much as see what's changing around me. I need to run. Maybe missiles' paths can later be mine. That way each path of mine cannot be barred, and can be as standard as my career path. The right path to Amériçaisian universal plutocracy is lined with legal tender for the rich, that's somehow portrayed as tenderNESS, and MINES for the poor to work in or walk on. I want to be behind bulky ballistic missiles, like I'm on the tail of an ambulance. That's being sure of some DIRECTION. I yearn to be staring at distressed, disfigured, wet, and vulnerable people about to collapse when trembling becomes an inadequate form of expression of slow death. Missiles may move fast but many people die slowly. This juxtaposition is what makes warfare memorable.

What is being placed sharply upon my long tongue? Sharply, I sharply feel that maybe my SHARP tongue can't be missed when SHARPLY against umami hands. It's so obvious as holes in such hands. I can imagine the outlines of spikes. The rough dorsum of my tongue could very well be flat and fertile land, and my BARK maybe could reflect my freedom of speech, should I choose to exercise it.

But I can't.

I can't scream or shout. My days of influential communication appear to be over.

This leaves a bitter taste in my mouth that I won't forget for as long as I live, like I'm a weaker person watching the weakest and voiceless people take their last gasps that are rather inaudible. There will be no accompanying last gasp of warfare.

✶✶✶✶✶✶

- SP: Scheer Post
Patrick Lawrence: The West—Technocrats, Incompetents, Ideologues
https://scheerpost.com/2022/10/02/patrick-lawrence-the-west-technocrats-incompetents-ideologues/amp/

["Is there a parallel between Liz Truss's inability to think and Washington's determination to prolong the fighting and dismiss all thought of a diplomatic settlement? Nothing too exact, but I see one. What Margaret Thatcher is to the British PM, America's ideology of invincible righteousness is to President Biden. The latter seems to be thinking through the ever-changing circumstances no more than the former. One feature of ideologies, after all, is they remove the necessity of rational inquiry. It is said here and there these days that Biden's foreign policy is the most aggressive and warlike of any in the postwar era. This may be so. To the extent it is, I read it as indicative of a paralysis—a sclerosis, maybe—that has been evident among the policy cliques for some time but now grows more acute. These people did not have to think after the 1945 victories.";

"The act of thinking had been forgotten. The resort has been to ideology and to nostalgia for a lost time."]

- Heinrich Böll Stiftung
War: Conflicts feed hunger, hunger feeds conflict
https://www.boell.de/en/war-conflicts-feed-hunger

- Discover
Technology
New Hope for Soldiers Disfigured in War
https://www.discovermagazine.com/technology/new-hope-for-soldiers-disfigured-in-war
["Some 40 percent of those severely wounded in Iraq and Afghanistan suffered devastating blows to the face."]

- VOA: Voice of America
Africa
Poverty Pushes Zimbabwe Miners into Underground, Dangerous Work, Observers Say
https://www.voanews.com/a/africa_poverty-pushes-zimbabwe-miners-underground-dangerous-work-observers-say/6199319.html

- The Conversation
Acid attacks are on the rise and toxic masculinity is the cause
https://theconversation.com/acid-attacks-are-on-the-rise-and-toxic-masculinity-is-the-cause-82115

- Forbes
Social Media
'Sleepy Joe' Trended After Biden Appeared to Nod Off During Climate Conference
https://www.forbes.com/sites/petersuciu/2021/11/01/sleepy-joe-trended-after-biden-appeared-to-nod-off-during-climate-conference/

- Al Jazeera
Opinion
Ameri-coup: A brief history of US misdeeds
https://www.aljazeera.com/opinions/2022/7/16/ameri-coup-a-brief-history-of-us-misdeeds

Chapter 16: Taste #2

My lips feel hot. Given incredible sensitivity, that's understandable. Lips are rich in nerve endings. Am I tasting any?

I'm rich. I know I am. Taxpayers pay my way into every prime location I go, while they themselves may stay put in slums. I work on behalf of contractors. Given important, vital, and satisfying warfare, such contractors freely spend citizens' taxes in the privacy of their own COMPANY. Yesteryear, every Amériçaisian taxpayer likely involuntarily put an average of the price of a nice flight toward the associated armed forces. Corporate contractors for the military were given nearly one in every two such dollars, as keen researchers like to highlight.

The taste of victory or defeat is similarly sweet for contractors so to match their forever rich lives of luxury. The consumption of bitters is welcome whenever. Bitter regret can only be felt by COMMON citizens, such as those whom relationships with surely turn sour. With enough rich military BASES around, the expression of acid excitement becomes satisfyingly SALTY. That's unpretentious but relatable to many powerful and soulless ideologues' experiences. Meaty men die and meaty books cover this. Money is forever made. Call the cool books UMAMITRATURE. There may be canons of genocide; warfare. There are rules on how to legally slaughter people. There may also be a umami canon. CANNONS can be on the ground, and may be parts of legs strewn across battlefields. Rich warmongers remain cool despite cool receptions. Expensive HOT bombs can be used to kill countless people regardless of how hot imaginations are. They may also be stolen goods. STEAMY carnage can be as hot as important issues, word of attacks, scents, women, and rhythmical metal to hear over screams. I'm very hot on this, like the selling of arms. Warfare is incredibly hot for business. Fighters aren't even hot enough for cops to chase. That's hot to handle but I handle it like a pro. Are things hotting up now? I can't tell.

Keeping expenditure of exertion and bucks up, is of foremost importance for foremost warmongers and lobbyists. Corporate death is an obscure aspect of corporate identity. Capturing funds like they're people, and vice versa, requires apt governance. Amériçaisian citizens may think that the two grand they involuntarily dish out annually to the armed forces, is some kind of life insurance, but it's actually death insurance; death assurance; assurance of death that honest people would offer with assurance. There is always an assurance that blood will be spilled. The firmness of intentions to wreak havoc mirrors the firmness of warmongers, stories promoting warfare, and hands on the hearts of others, before they're figuratively or literally ripped from CHESTS like cash.

I can taste something that must be sitting on my chest. But I don't need to get anything off it.

Death is as foreign as wars to civilians until carnage is on their dilapidated doorsteps, and few steps are taken by anyone. Even though the house always wins, it's very easy to gamble NOTES on warfare when certain SENTENCES are disregarded or unknown, like death and lines on diplomacy. I am keen on reading keen distress, fear, horror, and futility in faces, but only as a keen observer with keen eyesight, intellect, and such blades in hands. Keen winds and blasts enhance any coolness of keen carnage. Kids may keen over siblings, like vultures keening. Funding for warfare is hardly as keen as my sense of smell. Callous figures keenly bet on winners and wish for deaths. Certain FIGURES are loved lots, like DARK money. People have heads for them, and take heads OFF for certain FIGURES, like they're hats. Every TRIGGER FINGER is held up like it occurs; like soldiers stand to attention. You can't count profits or casualties on a single hand. But behaviors are impulsive like fighters and apparent choices, and hands are used repeatedly and keenly to all but skin silent souls.

FOREIGN FACILITATION that may be neuronal can be unnecessary. People can instead stop dead in their tracks before any careful diplomacy is exercised, no matter how exercised about carnage citizens are. Instead, profiteering is facilitated. Such facilitation gets right to the heart of the problem and squeezes it tightly until it stops beating, because there are no true pacemakers in making peace with people. Instead, pacemakers just stop running when it gets too difficult; the going gets tougher than they are. They drop to the ground ON THE GROUNDS that they can't properly GO ON. They're maybe dying AND in enemies' territory. Meanwhile, common peeps' water and funds can be siphoned into clean receptacles like sanitary FRUIT MACHINES. Oil and funds siphoned into similar receptacles are best used to improve warfare.

Owww!

My lips are burning. The unusual taste is sensational like cheap, fascinating, and fabricated stories about the delights of warfare for the victims.

Why can I taste so much blood?

Given money changing political hands, TRAILS of devastation may hardly be followed up, even when limbs trail in fluids, like I'm FEELING a little LIKE my tongue does. Do I FEEL like my tongue catching fire or the like? But it's not like me to stay so silent as it appears I will. People trailing behind others are forever slaughtered in the name of nations, like poor countries trailing behind richer ones. Arms forever trail behind better arms. Peaceniks trail behind in polls by large margins. The richest of the folk on campaign, nature, or tourist trails, or in the trail of a new film pushing warfare, are far enough from killing fields to always feel at home. They have the greatest influence over others with the least over anyone. The common voters and fighters are as insignificant as dust they can be hastily carved into after being trailed, and as their cries for help trail away. Associated magnificent arms are all the while thoroughly trailed. Trails simply stretch too far in opposite directions for the rich to ever notice the victims who beg to be heard. But I want to notice the needy, impoverished, distressed, and vulnerable children surrounded by metal arms, and use my own to wring their necks. I know how to follow trails, whether they're money, nature, campaign or killing fields.

I just need to wake up.

God bless Amériçaisia.

******

- Bill Gates Has WHAT Under All His Properties?!
https://youtu.be/JcHt2XSOQz8
["...facilitate the capture of wealth, whether that's something like a foreign war that allows taxes of ordinary people to ultimately end up in the hands of private military contractors..." - Russell Brand / Political Commentator]

- Institute for Policy Studies
National Priorities Project
Some Tax Day facts for 2022:
Tax Day 2022: We Got the Receipts
https://ips-dc.org/tax-day-2022-we-got-the-receipts/
["- The average taxpayer contributed about $2,000 to the military in 2021. Almost half of that went to corporate military contractors."]

- OtherWords
About That $900 You Gave Pentagon Contractors

https://otherwords.org/about-that-900-you-gave-pentagon-contractors/

- The Conversation
Lips are the most exposed erogenous zone, which makes kissing feel very good
https://theconversation.com/lips-are-the-most-exposed-erogenous-zone-which-makes-kissing-feel-very-good-34459

- Soma Blog
Human Lips are More Sensitive Than the Tips of Your Fingers
https://www.somatechnology.com/blog/fun-fact-friday/lips-are-more-sensitive-than-the-tips-of-your-fingers/

- Medikaur Skin & Aesthetics
11 Fascinating Lip Facts You May Not Know
2. Your Lips Are 100 Times More Sensitive Than Your Fingertips
https://www.medikaur.com/news/2020/12/10/11-fascinating-lip-facts
["Your lips have more than a million different nerve endings..."]

- The Atlantic
Ideas
America's Gambling Addiction is Metastasizing
https://www.theatlantic.com/ideas/archive/2021/11/world-our-casino/620791/

- Casino.org
Insider Insights
How Money Laundering Really Works & Why It's a Problem in the Gambling Industry
https://www.casino.org/blog/how-money-laundering-really-works/

Chapter 17: Smell #1

A smell's so funny that I would laugh if I could.

Not everyone can make as fine a living as dining, out of making arms. Sometimes they could be CUT, like smells through a nasal passage, without getting THEIR cut. Do naked arms even cut well? There may therefore be no clear point to the fighting in Ukraine. Weapons from Camden in Arkansas are used against Russians by Ukrainians, after being made decreasingly secretly behind trees and barriers. Now everyone knows about such gimmlers, guided missile launchers that are relatively light and mobile, and Javelin missiles. They're all on all screens. Gimmlers can be quickly fired in sixes, so six fresh PLUGS might be watched at once. Is that as fitting as a weaponized military butt plug? Other LAUNCHERS can be used too, like application ones. Folk can rely on ever-available gimmlers that can be used quickly and readily come rain or shine, to take out communities on surfaces just like where the launchers stand, some great distance away, fearful person by fearful person. They stand on the very same ground as perpetrators of war crimes. To think that they could have been friends.

I could fire Javelin missiles BY MYSELF like I personally made them. I could point them at victims, fire the missiles, destroy the peeps whether they're armed or not or even if they're in tanks, and forget that they ever even existed.

But I like when people do still exist for some short moment, and now I may prick my nostrils up like a tame prick as I think I smell the fear of those around me. Maybe I can take this well, lying down like I'm that well. Scents are beyond powerful. They're practically new MATERIAL. A smoky but gastronomic scent fills my nostrils like contractors filling me in on happenings; wonderfully rapidly. I feel accordingly energized despite my condition. I feel free.

An odor that's on the nose, in a sense, is certainly so sharp on my nose, in another sense, that I feel like my nose is falling off like scents could, NOW on the nose, in yet another sense, and this is all still right on the nose like direct people, mostly in senses as yet unused; overtly and perfectly experienced in a way that surely can't be on the nose; invalid when citizens are invalidated out of armed forces, but some people could find it on the nose in a less appealing way and astoundingly further sense. In short, I'm not smelling coffee because I'm still soundly comatose. Usually such offensive odors would keep people at bay like they're tanks or a deep DEPRESSION. But I cordially welcome people into MY valley when they smell this way.

I feel like I've been as stalled as my occupation and economic and military growth, for weeks on end. An attack on me has not been accordingly stalled, and now I lie in something akin to a stall. How many shiny ARMS drenched in tears can be placed in a small stall, like wealth above welfare; limits on movement; burdens on loved ones of the owners of such ARMS; in a position of vulnerability; under home stall arrest; under profound pressure; under the control of me alone? How many gimmlers and javelin missiles can be jammed so far up the pussies of female soldiers or asses of male ones, before they internally bleed to death while interned for periods as bloody aliens and foreign military doctors; combat medics? The missiles are like trees and fences being used against forces. There's no peaceful walk through woods, when some arms akin to hard wood are aimed at civilians by fighters surrounding them, and some missiles akin to wooden bullets are shot up their nether regions from nether regions like Camden in Arkansas, until parts of arms splinter in bodies like fighters into factions; until the citizens all end up with flakes of wood akin to splinters deep inside them like splints. They might initially have thought that an earthquake was destroying arms around them, until it was all too obvious that arms were to be hitting only them; until their last odorous breaths were expelled before they couldn't gasp for more.

Can I gasp for breath, or inhale breath that's salty like in like manner?

I can't hear my name being called, like I'm the loved one of a late soldier turning the volume down when said soldier's name's about to be mentioned on television, like the soldier's an indigenous Australian. Is it best that no one hears the name? The last name could be Grant, like that of an Indigenous Australian as obsessed as I am about armsmakers and defense, and pushing all this and more and more warfare as an appropriate think tank's senior fellow. Objectors be damned.

I value arms over the calmness of cities and people simply SOLEMNLY reading off names of the dead like they're rightly certain ever more lives will be lost. I would prefer to hear about just HOW they died. I would like for any associated ANNOUNCEMENT that includes egregious actions, to be as loud as a freight train passing by, so that loved ones are on their knees and incapacitated, before suffering the very same fate as specified. It's great to bring people down when they're up and entertained; to shock them the second they emerge from slumber in a sleepy town. Entire households may be named in the same breath as household names of arms, unless one lone member of a family is still alive to hear the announcement. Regardless, a deep breath may need to be taken by an announcer and listener alike. I would love for DEMONSTRATIONS to be more hands-on; for thousands of people to take to the streets in support of warfare when fully cognizant of the consequences of such associated bristling demeanors and determination. I want them to think of the bristling hairs on their face as weaponry as rigid as wartime bureaucracy, and experience a false sense of security and display bravado. I want to watch them from behind a fence in Camden where I'll see to it that they and their enemies all end up decapitated, when I can finally see again.

There are armsmakers, myself included, who are more keen for scenes to be made than money; keen profits. I just really don't want to BE the one being watched intently. There are so many poorer people to watch. In a version of my career that's not sanitized it would be made clear that I loathe sanitized rooms. Such is not the room I currently find myself residing in. Personally, I want to witness carnage right before my very eyes. And now I smell particulates that could exemplify the aftermath of such carnage. The smell of a body is intoxicating. This is the smell of capitalist industrialization; progress; death pollution; the largest weapons being used to make the smallest particulates. ARMS can be broken down like negotiations break down like lost souls. Barriers can be left up while psychopathy is expertly broken down instead, leading to some blissful societal breakdown as people suffer complete breakdowns. If there's piercing noise on the battlefield, however, this cannot be broken down. I can't break my current role down into anything more than simply taking this atmosphere all in right now. Am I turning my nose up at arms? I don't know. Can nurses be witnessing the incredible melting of parts of their own bodies as they stand before me gasping? Maybe they cannot repair damaged tissue. Their arms may be gone for good; up in smoke like dreams up in the air. My ARMS and aspirations are so much better. Any devastation is worth the price that's paid. The ingenious creation of smaller and smaller matter like microchips that can blow right into the brain through nostrils is simply phenomenal. People can even hold that thought.

I breathe in more particulates.

******

- Fall Out Boy - This Ain't A Scene, It's An Arms Race (Official Music Video)
  https://youtu.be/GNm5drtAQXs

- The Economist

Business │ Schumpeter

Despite Ukraine, these aren't boom times for American armsmakers

https://www.economist.com/business/2022/10/20/despite-ukraine-these-arent-boom-times-for-american-armsmakers

["The war in Ukraine has made it hard for Camden to remain low-key. Behind high fences and the forest canopy the armsmakers are assembling many of the weapons made famous by Ukrainians who use them to stall the Russian invasion. Javelin missiles, HIMARS guided-missile launchers and GMLRS rockets, known as "gimmlers", have become household names on tv and social media."]

- BBC News

Ukraine: What are Himars missiles and are they changing the war?

What is Himars?

https://www.bbc.com/news/world-62512681

["Himars - the M142 High Mobility Artillery Rocket System - is a missile launcher mounted on a five-tonne truck which can fire six guided missiles in quick succession."]

- Lockheed Martin

GMLRS: The Precision Fires Go-To Round

GMLRS Munitions: The right Precision Fires solution for every mission

Guided MLRS Specifics:

https://www.lockheedmartin.com/en-us/products/guided-mlrs-unitary-rocket.html

["Persistent, responsive, all-weather, rapidly-deployable, long-range, surface-to-surface, precision-strike capability;

- Fired from both the MLRS M270 family of launchers and the High Mobility Artillery Rocket System (HIMARS) launchers"]

- Lockheed Martin

Javelin

Javelin Weapon System

https://www.lockheedmartin.com/en-us/products/javelin.html
["Javelin is a single man-portable fire-and-forget medium-range antitank weapon system designed to defeat all known and projected threat armor."]

- Creative Spirits®
Aboriginal culture
People
Sorry Business: Mourning an Aboriginal death
https://www.creativespirits.info/aboriginalculture/people/mourning-an-aboriginal-death
["The Aboriginal tradition of not naming a dead person can have bizarre implications."]

- Stanford Graduate School of Business
Despite Costs, Outcome in Iraq Has Been Worth It Says Condoleezza Rice
https://www.gsb.stanford.edu/insights/despite-costs-outcome-iraq-has-been-worth-it-says-condoleezza-rice

- NITV: National Indigenous Television
The Point
Justice
Stan Grant: Australian and Aboriginal - the warrior who taught me how to be both
https://www.sbs.com.au/nitv/the-point/article/stan-grant-australian-and-aboriginal-the-warrior-who-taught-me-how-to-be-both/ztxu9qxi1

- WSWS: World Socialist Web Site
Student ejected from audience of Australian current affairs program for asking critical question on Ukraine
https://www.wsws.org/en/articles/2022/03/07/sgra-m07.html?pk_campaign=newsletter&pk_kwd=wsws

["In July 2020, Grant became a Senior Fellow at the Australian Strategic Policy Institute (ASPI), a right-wing think tank funded by the defence department and giant military hardware manufacturers..."]

Chapter 18: Smell #2

In my current state I can't talk to anyone to convince them to fight to their death.

In Russian regions, people can and do. Many people in Russia who are generally poor, in the minority ethnically, and residing in rural regions, are being forced to possibly die for Putin, according to some intelligence team looking into Russian conflict and media. In two weeks from around the end of September, a greater proportion of the respective eligible regional men, were recruited from poorer regions, with five-point-five percent of men from Krasnoyarsk Krai, where the average earnings every month are around two grand below the national average of forty four grand, who were eligible recruited; two-point-eight percent of men from Dagestan, where the average earnings every month are around fourteen grand below the national average, who were eligible recruited; zero-point-six percent of men from Ingushetia, where the average earnings every month are around twenty four grand below the national average, who were eligible recruited; zero-point-nine percent of men from Saint Petersburg, where the average earnings every month are around twenty two grand ABOVE the national average, who were eligible recruited; and zero-point-eight percent of men from Moscow, where the average earnings every month are around fifty grand ABOVE the national average, who were eligible recruited. The target for recruitment was one-point-two percent of the eligible male population nationwide.

I'm technically not a plutocrat. People like me are plural technocrats. I'm an ironically-singular and single plural technocrat, in another sense of the term PLURAL. I just love arms. Being a plutocrat in Russia, however, may be necessary for survival. The poor among the proletariat are forced to fend for themselves even on behalf of Putin. They would maybe even become armsmakers and psychopaths if given the opportunity.

I can imagine that finding the most unique people to persuade to put their lives on the line for their nation, is like smelling some odor that I've never smelled before. They're different enough to long to fit in or die trying. Notably, their sweat would have unique notes of molecules in it called odorants, mirroring notes of excitement in their voices, and likely not to be detailed in diplomatic or personal notes before their untimely deaths. I can't affirm the validity of this statement until I can again see those around me for myself. Are they here FOR me?

The trick is to make new recruits feel as though they're simply migrating to a new country to satisfy their wanderlust; lust for some new interesting BEAT, be it visible or mental; to influence happenings over beats of moments that in turn trigger them to want to go on dangerous adventures for the sake of seeking thrills without truly triggering them prematurely, as the production of the hormone of adrenaline is triggered when they're emotional, afraid, and/or excited, before intense pain is eventually triggered like rebellions being triggered off; before explosions trigger them repeatedly until they're beyond beat, without missing a fiercely emotional BEAT of warfare, or forceful explosive beat, like fiercely competitive foes. Their new heartbeats may be far less powerful than their last ones. They're simply deadbeats. The beat of war is excellent.

I smell bitter odorants.

When people are bitter enough, they're willing to fight anyone for their rights. They just have to be directed where to willingly go. That's why poor, bitter individuals uncritically go to war with those who are ultimately their peers; will not ultimately be their peers. It's akin to parents of children who are akin, angering one another to the point where they believe filicide is justifiable. Children are used as scapegoats. Domestic disputes become international. Adventures and wanderlust distract from domestic or local troubles. Perhaps the more local such initial troubles to speak of are, the more personalized any associated recruiting can be. Citizens are lured onto battlefields like they're studios in Hollywood, and feel like their personal problems now have international appeal. Talk is cheap and sweet. They get starstruck before being struck down, seeing STARS, and seeing their miserable lives flash before their insignificant eyes. The poorest are remembered by the least amount of people. No one listens to their cries in the best of times, let alone the worst. Many people in the poorest of communities like families, aspire to be TAKEN OUT for their country to be noted, at any cost to the point of in any sense. They aspire to be almost LOST and recapture lost youth if it has even been lost yet. This is akin to a nice night at a restaurant. A psychopathic recruiter goes on dates with prospective soldiers. They will eventually be LOST in faraway lands.

I smell some cuisine on myself. All ethnic cuisines smell bitter enough to mirror desperation, some drive that's mental or a recruitment one, and perhaps sexual drives.

The poorest people take it upon themselves alone to protect themselves against anyone who could soon be too CLOSE to them. Families are taken out rather than started. Poor people fear other poor people. They know just what they're capable of.

A smell is so bitter now; so much better now.

If running away from problems can be empowering, then soldiers can feel so powerful because in their minds they're like professional escapologists forever chasing dreams while CROSSING frontline workers, troops, and states like roads where there are just too many ways to look . . . at snipers, rather than helping any OPPOSING workers or troops who are already face-to-face cross WITH THEMSELVES like masturbating; walking right over the dead like water, like they think they're so much like Jesus that they'll survive themselves. They can surely CROSS parts of bodies like they're folding their ARMS; determined to succeed against all odds. Even bright suckers die on the FRONT LINE, no matter how qualified to save lives they are. Vulnerable nurses across ravines from fighters may CROSS OVER to fighters who themselves may cross over to ever more people, when getting popular, for life, if they can't pay their way to assured forever freedom rather than scenes of forever wars. They'll become such fighters themselves, or die trying; CROSSING OVER. They can be RANSOMED only once, then murdered before they ever have a chance to be ransomed for good. Donating a kidney is the least that poor people may think they're capable of. They believe they have to put their entire bodies on the line; FRONT-line. How could they possibly not believe this? So many people are clueless.

However, it doesn't pay to be smart. It only pays to be rich.

Smart psychopaths like me are only one in a hundred, or even fewer, so when smart people die this is usually a good thing from my perspective, because they were probably the ones interested in diplomacy rather than war. They're not the ones making enough money to protect themselves.

Peaceful areas may soon not be REMOTE from battlefields. All that's required is for me to get my own church and clubhouse in the midst of warfare and such a field, like traitors in the midst of fighters, from where I can control tanks and the like remotely as I observe carnage and the window I'm safely behind, like stark reality has been juxtaposed with safety that's of yesteryear for many fighters. I want bodies to pile up around me; to see bleeding faces pressed tightly up against the pane before me. I just hope that there are some holes in the glass so that I can smell the decomposing flesh of the fallen.

Now I can smell a rat; a smart doctor watching over me, whom I do want TO FIGHT[,] to save my life, but on a battlefield, and personally.

What does this doctor know about my psychopathic inclinations? Can she read my mind? What can I know about anyone when I can't properly sense them in more ways than one?

******

- Lenny Kravitz - Fly Away
https://youtu.be/EvuL5jyCHOw

- The Economist
Graphic detail | Daily chart
Where are Russia's newest soldiers coming from?
- Protect the wealthy [Chart]
https://www.economist.com/graphic-detail/2022/10/21/where-are-russias-newest-soldiers-coming-from
["Analysts suggest Mr Putin is relying on poor and remote areas of the country, often places with large ethnic-minority populations, to feed his faltering war machine (see chart).";
"Russia, selected regions % of eligible men called up to serve
Sep 21st-Oct 5th 2022";
"[Region:] Ingushetia; Dagestan; Krasnoyarsk Krai; St Petersburg; Moscow]";
"Average monthly income, roubles '000: [Approximately 20; Approximately 30; Approximately 42; "National average": Approximately 44"; Approximately 66; Approximately 94]";
[The "Mobilisation target level" was only met when recruiting men from Dagestan and Krasnoyarsk Krai.]
"Mobilisation target level [1.2]: 0.6; 2.8; 5.5; 0.9; 0.8";
"Source: IStories Media and Conflict Intelligence Team"]

- Taylor & Francis Online

Historical Studies
Volume 15, 1971 - Issue 57
Original Articles
The scapegoat theory of international war
I
https://www.tandfonline.com/doi/abs/10.1080/
10314617108595458?journalCode=rahs19
["...the belief that a troubled nation often wages war in the hope that
a glorious foreign adventure will allay unrest at home."]

- Squid Game
E07 - VIPS (2021, September 17)

- Psychologia
Visual
Infographic: Psychopath Vs. Sociopath
https://psychologia.co/psychopath-vs-sociopath/
["Psychopath": "1% of general population"]

- Exposed by CMD: Center for Media and Democracy
Featured Investigations
Defense Giants Spend Big on Lobbying and Elections to Boost
Post-9/11 Profits
https://www.exposedbycmd.org/2021/09/15/defense-giants-
spend-big-on-lobbying-and-elections-to-boost-post-9-11-profits/

- New Scientist
Real-life psychopaths actually have below-average intelligence
https://www.newscientist.com/article/2118547-real-life-
psychopaths-actually-have-below-average-intelligence/

- Healthline
Mental Well-Being
How to Tell if You're an Adrenaline Junkie

What is an adrenaline junkie?

https://www.healthline.com/health/adrenaline-junkie

["When you're excited, afraid, or emotionally charged, your body produces the hormone adrenaline."]

- M: Maples Family Law

Uncategorized

Are You Projecting Your Post Divorce Emotions onto Your Child?

https://www.maplesfamilylaw.com/uncategorized/are-you-projecting-your-post-divorce-emotions-onto-your-child/

- Learn Religions

Abrahamic / Middle Eastern >> Christianity

Jesus Walks on Water Bible Story Study Guide

https://www.learnreligions.com/jesus-walks-on-water-700220

Chapter 19: Sight #1

I'm stirring.

Will senators survive without me and my input? Will the coming together of Republican Jim Inhofe and Democrat Jack Reed be enough to ensure that the Department of Defense can legally get its hands on munitions, including artillery, for many years to come? Can they speak fluently enough to successfully propose such wartime privileges in a manner that ensures they are granted? Crucially, will there subsequently be a guarantee that stockpiles of arms of Amériçaisia can be replenished regardless of those competing against the Pentagon for contracts relating to the war in Ukraine? Billions must be spent by Amériçaisia. Money from taxpayers must be inordinately forthcoming. Arms made must outweigh Ukrainians' needs, as a hopeless hand that's a congressional soul told me such a proposal would ensure. False justification of absurdly and grossly excessive military expenditure is required, despite the value of it for the defense of ANY country being disputable. I'm told that the said proposal is a means to this end. Missiles that have a medium-range, are air-to-air, and are advanced, need to be obtained in the thousands numbering twenty, even though Ukrainians probably haven't even used them, and needn't. I'm told this can be accordingly ensured too. Amériçaisia needs ever more missiles than Ukraine wants. It's said that such stockpiles of arms are needed for a perversely FUTURISTIC ground war, not even against China. There are other arms to use against China.

I finally open my eyes.

I see flames.

I hear flames.

If I listen intently, I hear the crackle of such flames; CACKLES; CACKLES like the sound of people cackling on about whatever I can imagine in my wildest dreams, when and if they're not psychotically laughing at me.

I hear regular sharp notes that sound like sparks, like of ELECTRICITY, being sent my way, that might fly; like a woman telling me that I have a problem. I probably took note of that while comatose.

Was I arguing with fire then?

Perhaps I felt BURNT like being CUT, when burning like my face, with intrigue as a nurse BURNED fast by me, and her words deep into my heart, when I imagined the anthropomorphic flames saying that they couldn't be with me, perhaps to my deep relief. But was molten metal used when flames cast my hand in such relief from the very gurney I'm lying on, like all eyes being cast down on me; like hands truly being cast down? I need a cast now. My skin is melting, and hardly in relief against the gurney, and that's now being thrown into stark relief.

Did I truly hear a woman screaming as she burned to death? Did I mentally single out my organ of Corti when a flame touched it specifically? Was the body I dug my nails into my own gurney; some kind of coffin? Were my hands simply all over my very own skin? Was I the one struggling and gasping for breath; tossing about violently?

Was the heat of those around me actually the heat of flames? Were the screams and sharp cries ever more crackles of said flames like clouds open to interpretation when a person's using a single and specific sensory organ? Was the raspiness of a welcoming VOICE simply a reflection of the inhalation of smoke?

Sure, a nurse wondered aloud whether to save my life by hitting a button? Was it not the discharge lever of a fire extinguisher? Could I ever be discharged like pus? Perhaps I DID need immediate support? I still do! They probably couldn't tell if I had already been engulfed by flames or not?

But now I have opened my eyes as requested then. Or was the sensual and soft voice the sound of my soft skin sizzling into cordial like a drinkable atmosphere to take in like a fool or the sweep of a limb can? Was the act of bringing me into the world afresh akin to letting me die and go where I deserve to?

Yes, I very much felt metal against my skin. It was hot enough to melt. It was rubbing against my skin like both skin and metal were practically gel; some gum. My skin was being touched repeatedly by flames NIPPING at it, turning it all as sensitive as nipples. The heat was practically biting; biting me.

I once thought that the sensation of boiling water on itchy skin was pleasurable, but now similar pain is unbearable.

Flames lapping at my abdomen felt like a scalpel being jammed into it. They still might feel so.

Perhaps I felt a woman's skin brushing against mine moments before she let go of me and fled. Perhaps FREE hands were RUBBED IN MY FACE, but now I'm only a suffocating, immobile, and incapacitated sardine between flames.

Did I draw circles on my own skin? Did I feel my own dead skin against my live skin, that felt like a FOREIGN and exotic breast? My hairs indeed stood on end. I drew larger circles as the pain became ever more unbearable. Fingers curled up rapidly.

Indeed, something DID touch my tongue: a flame. A block tasted like an apple. Was it like an Adam's apple? After all, my cry came from the back of my throat. What came from the front? Perhaps nearby bitter sweets were on fire. I almost tasted them. Did I taste acid on my tongue? Then I tasted my own salty tears. Then I tasted MSG; my own skin! It was like chilis then gelato on my tongue. I tasted bitter fabric, felt wet myself, felt something sharp like nails against the dorsum of my tongue, then was left with a strikingly bitter taste in my full mouth.

My lips were so terribly hot. I imagined the taste of sweet victory, then thought about bitter regret and sour relationships. Was I simply EATING MYSELF UP over my past, like beating myself in such a manner?

I could easily imagine blood being spilled and chests being ripped open, because I was on fire that I couldn't possibly get off MY chest.

I almost felt my neurons catching fire; my heart being squeezed tightly. My lips were burning, and I tasted blood on blood.

The funny smell was of my own skin. Did I smell my own powerful fear, then gastronomic smoke? The smell of me was sharp and funky. I liked it at the time I didn't know what it was. I smelled my own breath and tears; death pollution; ever more particulates.

What I was now smelling was certainly unique; my own sweat when I had no control over how much I was sweating; an ever-bitter bitterer cuisine; decomposing flesh; a rat.

Now I see the source of everything that I can possibly sense; could have possibly sensed; flames engulfing me.

Now I can't even feel my own skin. My nerves have been scorched. It's as though I have undergone extensive neurotomies by fire rather than radio waves' heat. Pain signals are no longer being sent since nerves have been singed.

Now I really need those arms I've been dreaming about. I'll really need them if I survive this.

There's so much smoke that I can't possibly take a proper deep breath.

Are there even any flames here? Perhaps I'm hallucinating because of a lack of oxygen. Am I still comatose?

I don't know how many ARMS will be enough for me now. I need limbs; metallic limbs.

But most importantly, I need to get out of the room I'm in before the flames completely engulf me. I can't imagine the pain that could be caused by flames DIRECTLY LAPPING (at) my face; where nerves still exist. Actually, I almost can. I think about circles. Flames run laps around me.

I shudder at the very thought of more.

I can imagine being surrounded by ARMS. I can imagine being trapped and having nowhere to run to. I can certainly imagine an amendment to all my thoughts up to now, like an amendment to an ACT: the pain I and victims of war feel is so incredibly real.

I scream in distinct agony.

I sensed this coming.

Arms are like wars; walls. I'm trapped between such walls. I can't sit up because I'll pass out from smoke inhalation.

Is some DEFENSE simply insanity? Did I get myself into this situation? My defense may be resting now, if they have not yet been immolated. Where are all of my defenses? I can only justify fear and further rumination. I cannot justify any more immolation; military measures; national capital punishment of foreign or domestic civilians. My gurney's an electric chair I can't leap off, even when it's on fire; a pan; a kitchen I don't like the heat in. Will I BURN? Only an unbelievably maniacal psychopath moving impulsively and frenetically can generate the heat like that around me now. Was I simply moving myself?

Shockingly, I still have NERVES; some nerve, not fully comprehending the pain people feel yet. I feel the heat on the soles of my feet. Who has felt this before me? Who has walked over burning bodies; burning ARMS? Who has survived an explosion?

Have I previously proposed the crushing defeat of an army? I can see a mirror; contemplate a SHADY IMAGE of a warmongering being in the thick of some defeat; being in the thick of such defeat, as thick billows of smoke surround me; billow about; image of my political idols that I am; of some BLAZES to GO TO, as explosions blaze like guns; of senescence unlike youth; of destruction; of old armed forces; of life on a battlefield. Then there is the shady IMAGE of kin to think about like their apprehension, fear, confusion, doubt, anxious and indecisive suspense, and desperation, given DARKNESS and mystery. More arms equal less light. Trapped souls may lie all alone below rubble that's bone-crushing like an act can be.

I'm as stationery as I want military arms to be, because of crippling and debilitating fear.

Have I myself been TURNED ON through callousness? How could I possibly have been so simple? Am I now indeed being turned on?

Have arms been dropped on me? Have I been maliciously attacked repeatedly? Have people maybe TURNED ON arms in a court of law, like the arms are callous politicians? Has another domestic massacre taken place? Has a judge been blown up before they could gavel a verdict? Is a gavel itself dynamite? After all, what judge gets to actually decide whether to indiscriminately slaughter civilians? Judges may as well be redundant in a court of war. Do arms fall from skies like gavels of dynamite as makers of weapons make it rain torrentially and perpetually.

Personally, I was not safe behind closed doors.

Soon death will be ever CHEAPER. Perhaps it's already as cheap as possible. The Pentagon may not need to compete with any body to sell arms to another. They can be wholly behind the CHEAPEST slaughter. How could it possibly be any cheaper? Perhaps a soldier could butt others from behind, or use the butt of an old rifle to mangle many men, like a constitution. Psychopaths likely want to set records for body counts as swiftly and efficiently as possible. They kill enemy combatants and civilians they refuse to name, in cold blood and as blood runs cold. They may search for the easiest targets and breathe sighs of relief when kills are a breeze rather than a typhoon. They just can't help themselves when pleasing their superiors time and time again. Amassing arms could simply reflect uncertainty about the value of some TARGET for leaders hoping to distract citizens from such leaders' psychopathy; about valued targets' worth; target to maybe meet; values themselves. Who's a target for criticism; of proposals? What's a target? Who's a criminal? What can nuclear particles hit? Where exactly IS a target?

I'm sure that some red light is on my head. I SEE so much RED.

******

- Jerry Lee Lewis - Great Balls of Fire! (1957) 4K

https://youtu.be/F569_t2jCio

- Thought Russia Was Bad?! WATCH THIS!!
https://youtu.be/NeBdSxpFYNo

- Common Dreams
No Matter How Long the Ukraine War Lasts, Weapons Makers Plan to Cash In
https://www.commondreams.org/views/2022/10/20/no-matter-how-long-ukraine-war-lasts-weapons-makers-plan-cash

["A recent example of this came last week when Sens. Jack Reed (D-R.I.) and Jim Inhofe (R-Okla.) proposed a new amendment to this year's National Defense Authorization Act. The proposal would give the Department of Defense wartime powers that would free it to buy huge amounts of artillery and other munitions using multi-year contracts, according to Defense News. Here's the important part: the amendment would also authorize the Pentagon to skip competitive contracting for Ukraine-related deals (including billions of dollars' worth of contracts to refill U.S. stockpiles), and it would waive other provisions aimed at stopping weapons makers from overcharging taxpayers. As an unnamed congressional aide told Defense News, the move would allow contractors to produce far more than Ukraine needs.";

""It's part of the larger push to exploit the war in Ukraine to jack up Pentagon spending for things that have nothing to do with defending Ukraine, or any likely future scenario," Hartung said. As Defense News notes, the "proposed legislation also authorizes contracts for 20,000 AIM-120 Advanced Medium-Range Air-to-Air missiles, which Ukraine has not fired extensively – if at all." The package also includes purchases of several other missiles that seem to go far beyond Kyiv's wish list.";

""It's building stockpiles for a major ground war in the future," Mark Cancian of the Center for Strategic and International Studies told Defense News. "This is not the list you would use for China. For China we'd have a very different list.""]

- Mayo Clinic
Patient Care & Health Information > Tests & Procedures
Radiofrequency neurotomy
Overview
https://www.mayoclinic.org/tests-procedures/radiofrequency-
neurotomy/about/pac-20394931
["Radiofrequency neurotomy uses heat generated by radio waves to
target specific nerves and temporarily turn off their ability to send pain
signals."]

- Michigan State University
MSU Extension
Smoke inhalation is the most common cause of death in house fires
https://www.canr.msu.edu/news/
smoke_inhalation_is_the_most_common_cause_of_death_in_house_
fires

- Live Science
Near-Death Experiences Linked to Oxygen Deprivation
https://www.livescience.com/11010-death-experiences-linked-
oxygen-deprivation.html

- The Conversation
School shootings are already at a record in 2022 – with months still
to go
https://theconversation.com/school-shootings-are-already-at-a-
record-in-2022-with-months-still-to-go-192494

- Outlook
International
Gun Violence in America: 309 Mass Shootings Reported In 2022
https://www.outlookindia.com/international/gun-violence-in-
america-309-mass-shootings-reported-in-2022-news-206949

Chapter 20: Sight #2

It's not hard to believe that an officer recruiting Russian soldiers from and in Ust-Ilimsk was shot by a prospective soldier. That soldier was probably qualified to fight in a war against the national establishment. Those who are not qualified to really fight in any war are those who are inexperienced, are sick with a fever, have pneumonia or another disease, are mentally unstable, are old, or/and have not been medically checked. According to Russian soldiers, such people have indeed been recruited into some such armed forces. One journalist highlighting this, also stated that such men have more freedom of speech when death is potentially imminent; in trenches that are as grubby as dealing arms, and cops can't grab them like they would in a place they call home.

'This man was, for all intents and purposes, armed to the teeth with samples of arms he was pushing to legislators,' Tulsi Gabbard states.

What interesting PARTS he PLAYED.

Wait! Is she talking about me?

I crane my neck to see her on a television beyond a pane of glass that must be resistant to fire.

'He had them on him when he stepped into Franklin Park,' Tulsi continues. 'He was not, as some people claim, speaking out against the use of landmines and the like, like Princess Diana. What ever happened to truly moral royals, anyway? None since can beat her. Anyway, this man was peddling dangerous arms to anyone naive enough to hear him out. We know this from the people who wrote out against Hill Airy on Twitter. These are people who may have been censored by Twitter's former management. But Elon Musk is now in charge, no matter how much the national government does to limit his power. The elite can't have the national government stop the spread of new ideas, and limit free speech, so easily, when a progressive billionaire now owns Twitter. And we need to read about every true motivation for dealing arms because people like Hill Airy are not going to simply tell us what's going through their heads, not even on their deathbeds.

'People are now onto officials forcing them all to see, do, hear, read, and essentially sense, everything solely on officials' terms, in order to believe only what such officials tell them to throughout their entire lives, whatever they're up to, or suffer the consequences or/and get caught by the long arm of the law if not ARMS of the law.'

INSTABILITY is not a state to admire, but it IS memorable. Buildings become ruins. Fighting is CRITICALLY mental. Emotions run higher than smoke that victims of war cannot rise above, like word of friends' deaths. People should not get sick and grow old fighting all their life until they're murdered or actually become murderers. What about diplomacy? Are they not able to so much as talk? Powerful people on high horses in ivory towers simply close their windows. That's incredibly insensitive. They ride elephants in their rooms.

'Arrrrrgh!' I scream, as flames lap at my tissue, like it's paper I'm writing on. 'Help!'

Given INSTABILITY, nobody is about.

I'm using up ever more oxygen. I feel like I'm learning to breathe but can't get a grip on this or myself.

I'm not in a stable condition despite what my job was: very stable despite sadistic. Despite is done to victims of war by an industry that now earns MINE. Soldiers may kill soldiers, despite themselves. The relationship between different types of instability is ironically stable, and correlations are direct. It may be downhill from an easy declaration of war that there's gravity to, but it's all differently downhill from there. Civilians run DOWNHILL into throngs as dense as in Itaewon for Halloween. Any GRAVITY does not justify war crimes. Seriousness can be just as psychotic as silliness. Just because ARMS can hit the ground where they're needed does not mean they should always be required. There's far more to life than some simple GRAVITY. It takes a lot of skill to actually talk to people.

Seriously landing on top of foreigners should always be consensual. All fighters on battlefields are platonically raping their counterparts. Many are military virgins, but profusely and impolitely poke about in people where they don't belong. It's not even the place of experienced servicepeople to invade the personal spaces of others.

The instability before and during war is no different to the shocking instability of Seoulites in Seoul's Itaewon on the FATEFUL prophetic night surely before the storm of another mindless war orchestrated by insensitive and insentient psychopaths acting purely recklessly and impulsively. There are no safety nets on any horizon, just crushing defeats for every army, when push comes to shove. It's just too easy for everyone to run recklessly DOWNHILL.

People around the world seem to prefer fighting to getting on flights. That response leaves a lot to be desired, and many countries to still be visited.

There are no checks and checks and balances to ensure that diplomatic practices are undertaken; both promised to be adopted, and adopted.

Some military RANGE can be so close; in the range of a mile to a meter from a soldier's spot. However, plans for warfare may be too long-range. People just continue to get shot time and time again.

Maybe sometimes the freest a person feels is when they're just about to die. It may have never been their intention to feel so free at such a time, but suddenly they truly have nothing to lose by speaking their mind; tweeting what must not be censored. Maybe the greatest gift a soldier can give to a foreign counterpart is exposure through the proficient distribution of their last words; to pass a microphone to a foe, if not a rose. Some simple POST is not great enough to symbolize a goalpost. Soldiers should let everyone see every POST. What need is there for private POSTS but for planning secretive military executions? People whom other people presume are absent- and unlike-minded are rounded up and taken out, whether near or far from posts. That's warfare. When all POSTS are not seen, all lips are not read like tweets; all agony is not comprehended; all suffering is forgotten. When WikiLeaks is not leaking, then people think that everything is SOLID; sound; reliable; reliable like some SUPPORT that's emotional; financial; human; to the idea that war in necessary; reliable like some DEFENSE, and psychotic wartime actions. There's always a LEAK to look for in a PIPE dream. But citizens and victims of war all see lives flash before their eyes bereft of such dreams. They cry out in opposition to the warmongering elite that callously PUT THEM IN THEIR PLACES.

Their final utterances are sadly MISSED.

No one can hear ME now.

'Arrrrgh!' I cry.

I can barely breathe in anything but smoke.

I gasp for the necessary twenty one percent of oxygen in air inhaled. I'm almost OUT OF IT when now breathing in air that's only maybe seventeen percent oxygen.

It's fifteen percent oxygen.

I take another breath.

It's ten percent oxygen.

I'm going to pass out.

I leave my ARMS to no one, not even science.

******

- Flobots - White Flag Warrior ft. Tim McIlrath
https://youtu.be/Lsgbb23z27w

- Hozier - Swan Upon Leda (Official Lyric Video)
https://youtu.be/LKroEZ9vVyw

- Elton John - Candle in the Wind/Goodbye England's Rose (Live at Princess Diana's Funeral - 1997)
https://youtu.be/1o9rLDCfO6o

- We As Americans [- Eminem]
https://youtu.be/tbUEkqcY0oU

- Mosh (Dirty Version) by Eminem | Eminem
https://youtu.be/9wRLd5l7WYE

- Flobots - Handlebars (Official Video)
https://youtu.be/HLUX0y4EptA

- PBS News Hour

Russian military recruiter shot at enlistment office amid troop call-up

https://www.pbs.org/newshour/world/russian-military-recruiter-shot-at-enlistment-office-amid-troop-call-up

["A young man shot a Russian military officer at close range at an enlistment office...";

"In the attack in the Siberian city of Ust-Ilimsk..."]

- Inside Russia's Military Collapse | Super Users

https://youtu.be/XATbBXqwKx4

["They recruit, actually, everybody - old people, sick people, people without any military experience." - Mark Krutov / Investigative Journalist;

"There was no fucking medical commission at all! There are mentally unstable people here." - Anonymous Russian Soldier;

"People are sick! Pneumonia, diseases, fever..." - Anonymous Russian Soldier;

"It's one thing when you are at your home city, and if you say something, police will come after you. But when you are sitting in the dirty trench, and you can die at every next second, maybe you're just feeling a little bit more free [to post]." - Mark Krutov / Investigative Journalist]

- THIS Is Why Musk's Twitter Takeover Matters - Tulsi Gabbard

https://youtu.be/YyT3ZKbVRzM

["What's dangerous about what's happening here with Elon Musk continuing to forge ahead very correctly in his commitment to free speech and how he wants to change Twitter to be a truly free marketplace of ideas, the power elite are so threatened by it that they are launching the muscle of the federal government against him." - Tulsi Gabbard / Former United States Representative;

"...more and more people are opening their eyes to, you know, Big Brother, big government intruding into just about every parts [sic] of our lives, and dictating to us what we can and can't do, what we can and can't read or see or hear or believe with the force of law and really serious consequences coming behind it." - Tulsi Gabbard / Former United States Representative]

- Town & Country Magazine
Society > Heritage
Why Princess Diana's Fight Against Landmines Was So Remarkable
https://www.townandcountrymag.com/society/tradition/a12021518/princess-diana-landmines/

- AIS Glass
How Can Fire Resistant Glass Improve the Safety of Your Building?
https://www.aisglass.com/fire-resistant-glass-improve-safety-building/

- NewsNation Now
Smoke inhalation most common cause of death in house fires
https://www.newsnationnow.com/morninginamerica/smoke-inhalation-house-fires/
["The primary way smoke inhalation kills is through suffocation from a lack of oxygen. A 21 percent oxygen level is considered normal. At 17 percent, there are impairments, and at 9 percent, people can go unconscious."]

- UTS: University of Technology
Surgical and Anatomical Science Facility
Body Donation Program
Why donate your body to science?
https://www.uts.edu.au/about/faculty-science/surgical-and-anatomical-science-facility/body-donation-program

- 7 News

Government working to determine if Australians involved in South Korean Halloween stampede disaster

https://7news.com.au/news/disaster-and-emergency/stampede-kills-at-least-146-during-halloween-parade-in-seoul-c-8699129

- Bankrate

Investing

Elon Musk in 2022: What to know about the world's richest person

https://www.bankrate.com/investing/elon-musk/

- WikiLeaks

https://wikileaks.org/

Bonus Unrelated Piece: Squid Ink

'Why did you choose me?' Sooji asks, pouring Matthew a glass of water.

Matthew is sitting cross-legged on the heated wooden floor of Sooji's apartment in Maebong. His arms are stretched out behind him, and palms flat on the floor.

'What do you mean?' Matthew replies.

'Why did you pick me to meet?' Sooji presses. 'I have no references on Couchtapper. How did you know you could trust me?'

Matthew shrugs, and glances at Sooji.

'You looked trustworthy,' Matthew states.

'Because I am female?' Sooji asks. 'I am a tough female, Matthew. I am not like the other women you have met. It's hard to be a strong feminist in Korea. Everyone looks down on me because I am thirty and not married. So, I am very bitter inside. I am not the average Korean . . . chick? Is that what you Australians say?'

Matthew laughs.

'We do, but we don't say it as cute as you do,' Matthew says.

'I am not cute,' Sooji says, walking over to Matthew with two glasses of water.

Matthew looks around.

'Oh yeah,' Matthew says. 'I don't see any mirrors. You mustn't know what you look like.'

'Cute are the absurdly white K-pop idols,' Sooji says. 'They look like Hello Kittens. I am not a kitten. You cannot buy me at a pet store.'

Sooji hands Matthew a glass of water that he sits up straight to take cordially, like it's cordial.

'I'm sorry this is all I have,' Sooji says. 'I didn't think you would be coming home with me.'

'It's perfect,' Matthew says.

'It's not perfect,' Sooji says. 'It's water. If you go to a restaurant, you do not want to be served water.'

'I drink water at restaurants,' Matthew says.

Sooji looks at Matthew, and puts her own glass down in front of him.

'Do you like tea?' Sooji asks.

'It's okay,' Matthew says.

'Hmmmm,' Sooji says, pouting a little.

'Do YOU like tea?' Matthew asks.

'I pick tea in Jeonnam where my parents live,' Sooji says. 'I want to make you some, but not if it is just meh to you.'

'I would LOVE to have some,' Matthew says. 'It's very special because YOU picked it. But I don't want you to use too much. I'm only a visitor.'

Sooji nods.

'Good,' Sooji says. 'Don't get attached to me. Don't be a tea bag on a string. But you are not just a visitor, Matthew. We kissed many times. I do not kiss all my visitors.'

Matthew smiles.

'They were the best kisses I've ever felt,' Matthew states.

Sooji turns around and picks up a tea cup and strainer.

'You're lying,' Sooji says.

She puts the strainer in the tea cup, then picks up a saucer, like preparing MORNING TEA well into a night. Australians would make a meal of it.

'I'm really not,' Matthew states.

Sooji puts the saucer below a tea cup holding a strainer, onto the floor.

Sooji stares at Matthew.

'How many Asians have you kissed before?' Sooji asks.

'You're the first,' Matthew says.

'Ha,' Sooji says, rolling her eyes. 'Then no wonder they're the best kisses you've had. But the moment you kiss another Asian woman,

THAT will become the best kiss. You like it because it's exotic. I'm nothing special, Matthew. Really.'

Sooji stands up and walks toward a kettle, like preparing to burn (insult) herself, but that's so laughable that she could be taking the stage at an international comedy gala.

'You are perfect, Sooji,' Matthew says.

'Stop it,' Sooji replies. 'Don't patronize me. You are an author. You write about women all the time. I am the inspiration behind just ONE page in your latest book. I can't show you everything there is to see in Korea. You will want to meet more women. They will show you more than I can. I can only serve you tea. It is all I have.'

Sooji hits a button on her kettle.

'Soon you will hear the kettle whistle like a typical man,' Sooji says, shaking her head.

'I really love where you took me today,' Matthew says. 'Gonggung Palace was beautiful.'

'GYEONGBOKGUNG Palace,' Sooji corrects Matthew. 'You were bored. You started making jokes to amuse yourself.'

'I'm so sorry,' Matthew says. 'I was just trying to cheer myself up because I knew you had to go to work, and I wouldn't see you again until tonight.'

The kettle whistles.

'Is that true?' Sooji says over the whistle. 'I want to show you things here that are remarkable. I want you to truly experience Korea, and be impressed.'

'I want that,' Matthew says. 'That would be amazing.'

The kettle stops whistling. Sooji picks it up and takes it to Matt.

She places it before him.

'This has to cool down,' Sooji says. 'Or the tea will get burned. It's like a hyperactive kid who should be insulted.'

'Smart,' Matthew says. 'COOL DOWN is essentially a homonym. I use them all the time in my writing.'

'I am smarter than you think,' Sooji says. 'I am not a typical Korean chick.'

'I know,' Matthew replies. 'But Korean women ARE typically smart.'

Sooji opens a drawer and picks up a bag of tea from inside it.

'Now I'm a drug dealer,' Sooji states.

A card falls to the floor. It's brown with a black circle, triangle, and square on it.

'What's this?' Matthew asks, picking it up.

'My sister gave me that before she went off to be a contestant on a game show,' Sooji answers. 'It's like that Big Sister show, I think. I haven't heard from her because she wasn't allowed to take her cell with her.

She's been on the show for a while now. It should be on television soon. Maybe she won.'

'Wow,' Matthew says. 'That's pretty sweet.'

'So, what do you want to see in Korea?' Sooji asks, sitting down in front of Matthew and placing the bag of tea by the kettle. 'What foods do you want to try?'

'Well, I've tried yakgwa,' Matthew says.

'Sweet medicine,' Sooji says, smiling. 'More drugs.'

Matthew laughs.

'I've tried bibimbap,' Matthew continues. 'I've been to Gong . . .'

'GYEONGBOKGUNG Palace,' Sooji finishes.

Matthew smiles and nods, putting his glass down and hands in his lap.

'I've seen the Namsan Tower,' Matthew says. 'I've seen a traditional apartment.'

'You've felt ondol,' Sooji says.

'What's that?' Matthew asks.

'That's the traditional underfloor heating,' Sooji says.

Sooji gently takes Matthew's hands in hers.

'Where can I take you?' Sooji asks. 'I want this to be your best trip ever. You travel to two countries every year, but I want you to never forget Korea. What can I show you?'

'Sooji, just being with YOU makes this my best trip ever,' Matthew says.

Sooji shakes Matthews hands like his arms are battle ropes.

'Matthew,' Sooji says, sternly. 'Stop it. You know I can't even fuck you because I am having my period.'

'Sooji, kissing you is perfect,' Matthew says. 'It's pure bliss.'

Sooji sighs.

'Tell me what to do,' Sooji presses.

Matthew picks up the card, with Sooji's hand still holding his.

'How did your sister get on this show?' Matthew asks.

'She rang the number on the back,' Sooji says. 'Why?'

'Do you think it's like a Korean Big Sister?' Matthew asks. 'Maybe I can learn all about Korean culture on the show.'

Sooji laughs.

'You can't compete in a game show here,' Sooji says. 'You don't even know Korean. Can you even remember hangul, Matthew? What is M for Maeteu?'

'A square,' Matthew says.

'A rectangle,' Sooji replies.

'That's splitting hairs,' Matthew quips.

Sooji runs some fingers through her hair.

'That is so cute,' Matthew says, smiling.

Sooji lets go of Matthew's hand then snatches the card off him. She flips it over to look at the back.

'Let's do it,' Sooji says. 'You'll need a translator. I'll play it with you. I can show you that I'm more than just a chick.'

Matthew shrugs.

'Are you sure?' Matthew asks. 'I already know you're special.'

'Yeah,' Sooji replies. 'But this might be fun.'

******

- Tove Lo - 2 Die 4 (Official Music Video)
https://youtu.be/eUSkZCoGalo

- Squid Game (2021)
Season 1

Lightning Source UK Ltd.
Milton Keynes UK
UKHW041906111122
412065UK00013B/213/J

9 781685 835743